translating the good news through teaching activities

DONALD L. GRIGGS

A Griggs Educational Resource

published by
Abingdon / Nashville

Abingdon Edition 1980

Second Printing 1980

Copyright, 1973, GRIGGS EDUCATIONAL SERVICE

All rights reserved. No part of this book may be reproduced (worksheets and maps excepted) in any form without permission in writing from the publishers. For information write Abingdon, Nashville, Tennessee.

The Bible texts in this publication are from Today's English Version of the New Testament. Copyright © American Bible Society 1966, 1971. Used by permission.

ISBN 0-687-42527-1

Foreword

This book has been in the process of being written for almost two years. Most of the activities and resources described in these pages have been used many times in workshops with teachers and classes with students. In planning my Summer of 1973 I decided to decline all invitations for workshops in May and June and to spend that time putting the finishing touches to this book.

There are many persons who have attended workshops throughout the country who have given helpful evaluations and suggestions of the activities and resources in the book. To each one who may eventually read this book and find something familiar I say "thank you." In addition to these nameless persons I am especially indebted to several other very special persons.

Miss Annie Vallotton was very gracious to respond to my request of her to create an original line drawing for the cover. In the midst of a very busy schedule from one end of the country to another she took time to create the line drawing that appears on the cover. I received the drawing on the back sheet of hotel stationery. Needless to say that piece of paper will always be a treasure. In addition to the line drawing Annie wrote two very encouraging letters. In one letter she added these words:

> "People of our days are most accustomed to very quickly catch hold of an idea on a wall (poster advertising) or in a magazine or on television (commercials). I do believe that a very simple line is attractive and will appeal to everybody, giving the maximum of expression with a minimum of lines. I really think that it is a need to eliminate each line which is not indispensible so as to retain the main ones. To me it is fascinating to do so. A good exercise to accomplish this is to ask somebody to place himself in a chosen posture from which you can draw. This method already gave very good results when used in Sunday schools."

Thank you very much Annie! Also, a "thank you" to the American Bible Society for graciously permitting me to use many line drawings and scripture verses from Today's English Version of the New Testament.

In addition to Annie Vallotton's line drawings I have several chapters that have been illustrated by another very talented artist who is also a good friend and neighbor, Mary Corman. Mary has illustrated three of our other books and always seems to catch the essence of what is intended. I am very appreciative of Mary's creativity.

For other books my wife, Pat, did all of the typing of the rough draft and finished manuscript. While I was doing this book Pat was busy working on her own book on Creativity Activities, keeping the business going and being mother and wife. So I am thankful for the many hours of typing by Barbara Owen, another friend and neighbor. Barbara's excellent typing allowed the printers to set type and send me a finished copy to proofread which speeded up the publication date.

From Livermore, California, to wherever you are all of us who have contributed to the production of this book wish you success in your work of translating the Good News to students in your class.

Donald L. Driggs

July 2, 1973

TRANSLATING THE GOOD NEWS THROUGH TEACHING ACTIVITIES

TABLE OF CONTENTS

Introduction		1
Ways To Use This Book		2
One:	Individual or Small Group Reading For Information	3
Two:	Start With the Word List	4
Three:	Start With the Index	7
Four:	Start With the Cross Reference Notes	8
Five:	Twenty Ways to Use The Line Drawings	9
Six:	Focus On One Gospel — Mark	19
Seven:	Focus On The Acts Of The Apostles	27
Eight:	Focus On An Epistle — Ephesians	41
Nine:	Using T.E.V. With Values Clarification Strategies	50
Ten:	Use The Overhead Projector With T.E.V.	55
Eleven:	Use The Cassette Recorder With T.E.V.	65
Twelve:	Use The Slide Projector With T.E.V.	73
Thirteen:	Use The Filmstrip Projector With T.E.V.	77
Fourteen:	Use The 16mm Projector With T.E.V.	83
Fifteen:	Use The Thermal Copier and Spirit Duplicator With T.E.V.	91
Bibliography		97

Translating The Good News Through Teaching Activities

Introduction

Good News For Modern Man* is a recent translation of the New Testament published by the American Bible Society. The T.E.V.* was originally intended for persons for whom English is a second language or who were identified as functionally illiterate. The fact is, T.E.V. has become the all-time best seller in the paper-back category of books in general and of the Scriptures in any form. The T.E.V. has become popular with young and old with all degrees of reading ability. Perhaps it is because the language of the Scriptures is a "second language" for everyone that this translation has become so widely used.

An argument came up among the disciples as to which one of them was the greatest. Jesus knew what they were thinking, so he took a child, stood him by his side, and said to them "The person who in my name welcomes this child, welcomes me; and whoever welcomes me, also welcomes the one who sent me. For he who is least among you all is the greatest."

Luke 9:46-48

The American Bible Society has been in the business of translating Scriptures into the languages of the world in order for persons to be able to read and hear for themselves the Good News in words they understand. One of the major arenas for translating the Scriptures on the American scene is in the classrooms of all the churches where teachers and students are engaged in meaningful study of the Bible.

One of the primary roles of the church teacher is that of *translator*. In a very real sense the teacher is a translator as he stands between the *student*, with his language and world view, and the *Bible*, with its own language and world view, in order to facilitate communication and understanding. The teacher as translator seeks to use a variety of means and media in order to assist the student in his exploration of the rich heritage of Scripture. The teacher needs to use the latest translations of Scripture, but also must supplement those translations with teaching and learning activities and material resources in order to involve students with all their interests and abilities.

When they approach Scripture, students are functionally illiterate when it comes to interpreting or responding to the language of the Scripture. Students can be motivated to study and appropriate to themselves the truth and meaning of the Bible when they can make sense out of the process of their study and when they can enjoy what they are doing.

---

*Today's English Version of the New Testament (T.E.V.) published by the American Bible Society, 1966.

What follows in this book is a series of suggestions and outlines for using T.E.V. and related resources as integral components to the study of Scripture in the church classroom. The suggestions presented here are intended to be illustrative of what is possible with a variety of other parts of Scripture. These suggestions can be used with any students who are able to read at a level intended by the T.E.V. Often a particular part of T.E.V. is used as the focus and other resources are recommended.

So Jesus said to the twelve disciples, "And you — would you like to leave also?" Simon Peter answered him, "Lord, to whom would we go? You have the words that give eternal life. And now we believe and know that you are the Holy One from God."

There are other resources included in a Bibliography at the back of this book. Even though the focus is New Testament and the specific translation is T.E.V. it is possible the basic principles, approaches, and resources could be applied to other parts of the Bible and with other translations. Some teachers who have seen the rough draft of this book have thought that what is included here could be used as a course of study with a class desiring to study the New Testament.

WAYS TO USE THIS BOOK

There are some other ways I see that this book can be used:

1. A teacher who wants to focus on the New Testament in his teaching could use this book as a guide for preparing his lesson plans.

2. A teacher may use a section like the one on *Acts of the Apostles* exactly as written as the curriculum for one unit.

3. A church educator could use two or three of the activities suggested here as models for teachers to experience directly in a teacher training session.

4. Putting the book *20 New Ways of Teaching the Bible* and this book together with *The Planning Game* some creative teachers could write their own curriculum.

5. Many of the resources and activities suggested in the book could be used as the basis for learning centers where teachers want to increase student choices and involvement.

6. Some of the activities and resources could be used in vacation church school and church camp settings.

7. A number of the activities could be selected for use in a multi-age, open classroom learning situation.

There are other ways to use this book. You will discover some that work and others that do not. Be creative! Try some new ideas that you think of as a result of reading the suggestions here. Let us know how it works!

—2—

One: Individual Or Small Group Reading For Information

We have all used the Bible by ourselves or in small groups. The most obvious approach of the teacher is to have students read a specific passage of Scripture, then to use that passage as a basis for class discussion. This is an often-used technique but is limited in its value for effective teaching and learning. Because the technique of assigning a passage to read or the teacher reading it orally has been used so often, the students are bored and unmotivated to respond to this approach. Especially in an era when persons are becoming less and less print oriented there is increased need for using more creative approaches and adding other media that will more effectively involve students in the process of their own learning.

One way to increase the effectiveness of this approach to studying and discussing the Bible is to instruct students to look for something specific as they read. By having a question or a key concept to focus their attention, the students will be more actively involved in their reading. Once when I was doing a "Creative Ways to Teach the Bible Workshop," a participant came to me during the coffee break with the comment, "I belong to a Bible class in our church. This week we were to read ten chapters in the Book of Isaiah. I read the chapters but I didn't understand what I read. So I read them again. I still do not understand what I have read. What's wrong with me?"

Your faith, then, does not rest on man's wisdom, but on God's power.

I Corinthians 2:5

It is really too bad that the teacher thought there was something wrong with her. I asked her, "What were you reading those ten chapters for? She did not understand my question so I stated it a second time. Her answer was, "I don't know. I guess we are going to discuss those ten chapters next week."

The dialogue with this person illustrates the problem with just assigning passages to be read. If the teacher of that class had provided a question or two, or had offered a few key concepts to search for, I am sure his students would have felt more capable and involved in the assignment. I believe that when students are assigned something to read, or listen to, or view, that they should have a reason for doing it and they should be aware of the reason.

Two: Start With The Word List

WORD LIST

Council The supreme religious court of the Jews, composed of seventy leaders of the Jewish people and presided over by the High Priest.

Covenant The agreement that God made with Abraham (Genesis 17.1–8), and later with the people of Israel (Deuteronomy 29.10–15).

Cummin A small garden plant whose seeds are ground up and used for seasoning foods.

D

Dalmatia The southern half of the province of Illyricum.

Dedication, Feast of The Jewish feast, lasting eight days, which celebrated the restoration and rededication of the altar in the Temple by the Jewish patriot Judas Maccabeus, in 165 B.C. The feast began on the 25th day of the month Chislev (around December 10).

Defile To make dirty, or impure. Certain foods and practices were prohibited by the Jewish Law because they were thought to make a person spiritually or ceremonially unclean. In this condition such a person could not take part in the public worship until he had performed certain rituals which would remove the defilement.

Demon An evil spirit with the power to harm people, that was regarded as a messenger and servant of the Devil.

One of the unique features of T.E.V. is the *Word List* which appears in the back of the book. In doing workshops where I have directed persons to turn to the *Word List* I have encountered many surprised looks on person's faces who, though they were very familiar with T.E.V. never were aware of the *Word List* in the back. This *Word List* contains many of the key words of the New Testament and includes a brief definition or explanation of each. There are 168 words included in this section of T.E.V.

Teachers can instruct students to read a definition of a key word to be studied in the class period, then to make a list of questions about a key word. Some other resources like Bible Dictionary, Word Book, Encyclopedia, Concordance, Commentary and Atlas should be available to do some searching for answers and additional interpretations of the key word.

Teachers and students could develop their own word lists of key words not included in the T.E.V. list. These special words could be kept in a notebook, or on a chart, with brief definitions written in the teacher's or student's own words. Developing a working vocabulary is a very necessary skill for increasing Biblical literacy.

A SUGGESTION . . . focus on the word *DISCIPLE*

** Instruct students to look up the word "disciple" in the *Word List* and read the brief definition:

> *"A person who follows and learns from someone else. The word is used in the New Testament of the followers of John the Baptist and Paul; it is especially used of the followers of Jesus particularly of the twelve apostles."*

** Then, based on that brief definition, ask students to state what questions come to mind about the word "disciple" and its definition.

** The students may express a wide variety of questions:

1. What is the difference between disciple and apostle?
2. Who were the twelve apostles?
3. Does a disciple just follow and learn?

4. Are there disciples today?

5. How does a person get disciples to follow him?

6. Who were the disciples of John the Baptist and Paul?

7. Is the word "disciple" used only in the New Testament?

** The important thing is that the questions be the students' own questions. The number that is asked is not important. It is also very important that the teacher receive and record the question just as the student stated it. It is possible for the teacher to state a question or two if something important is being overlooked.

** After allowing time for students to think of and state their questions, provide resources for them to use in order to pursue the answers to their questions. The least helpful thing a teacher could do is to answer the questions for the students.

** Encourage students to start with any question they want and to use whatever resources they choose. Allow sufficient time and be sure there is a variety of resources available so that students will have success in finding answers to their questions. Some possible resourses are suggested in the Bibliography.

As Jesus walked by Lake Galilee, he saw two fishermen, Simon and his brother, Andrew, catching fish in the lake with a net. Jesus said to them, "Come with me and I will teach you to catch men." At once they left their nets and went with him.

Mark 1:16-18

There are several very basic educational principles that are operative in an activity such as what is outlined above. These principles can be applied to any age group and any portion of Scripture.

1. The students are guided to *focus on one concept*. Many times when we start with a long passage of Scripture to begin our study we encounter so many concepts that the students are overwhelmed and confused. By starting with a key concept we focus the students' attention and provide time and resources for exploring the concept in sufficient depth so it may become a meaningful part of their vocabulary and experience.

2. The students are more *motivated to investigate their own questions* than they are the questions of the teacher. When the student states a question that becomes "property" of the whole class, then he has something "at stake" in what will happen. If the teacher asks all the questions, then the teacher is the only one who has anything "at stake." When students invest something of themselves, then they are more motivated to participate further in the class activities.

3. The students' *questions are accepted and recorded* by the teacher *just as they were stated*. When teachers edit what students say and write something else in their own words, then they are in effect saying, "I have thought about this more than you have and I know more about it than you do. When you have as much knowledge as I have then you will say it this way." We would never say that in so many words, but our actions say it for us when we change what students say or write. We can help students rethink what they have said. If we offer something in addition to or different than what they said, then we should get their permission to write it down. If we want students to hesitate or withdraw in their participation, then all we have to do is continually edit their contributions. On the other hand, if we want to encourage and reinforce their participation so that they will feel free to participate again, then we will help them by receiving what they contribute.

4. The students are *able to select* the questions they wish to pursue. The more choices a student has in the course of his study, the more motivated he will be to participate in his own learning.

Three: Start With The Index

The section immediately following the Word List is the *Index*. The *Index* includes 262 words with many page references for the key words. Some other editions of the Bible include abbreviated concordances, but this is the only translation I know of that has such an *Index*. All the major person and place names are included.

As in using the Word List as a starting place it is helpful to focus on a key concept or category by starting with a word in the *Index*.

** Start with a word like "Parable" or "Miracle" and instruct students to select one parable or miracle to look up, read, study and discuss. It would be helpful to have some additional resources available.

** Select a person to study and start with the references next to the name to find out more information about the person. Each student can select a different name and then compare notes after the research.

** Start with a word like "Jesus," "Peter," or "Paul" which have many references. Divide the references among the students to do separate research; then compare notes.

INDEX

A
Aaron 284, 490, 493, 496
Abel 60, 170
Abraham 5, 183–184, 233–234, 345–346, 422–424, 502–503, 512
Adam 347–348, 396, 397, 468
Aeneas 291
Agabus 296, 321
Agrippa *see* Herod Agrippa
Ananias
  of Damascus 290, 324
  High Priest 325, 328
  Ananias and Sapphira 278–279
Andrew 7, 115, 213, 224, 243
Anna 137
Annas 139, 256, 276
Antioch
  of Pisidia 300–303
  of Syria 296, 299, 304–305, 307, 421
Apollos 314–315, 374, 375, 399
Apostles 22, 85, 148, 269, 542, 574

"Benedictus" 134
Berea 311
Bernice 330–331
Bethany
  near Jerusalem 53, 66, 117–118, 239–243
  beyond Jordan 212
Bethlehem 2–4, 135–136
Bethphage 51, 108, 191
Bethsaida 26, 95, 100, 159, 213
Bethzatha 221
Blood 68, 119, 200, 201, 226, 262, 386, 388, 389, 496, 497, 498, 500, 503, 506, 507, 508, 517, 530, 536, 553, 560, 565, 566, 569, 570, 571
Bread
  material 6, 39, 40, 95, 209, 267
  spiritual 225–226
  offered to God 27, 84, 147, 496
  Lord's Supper 67–68, 119, 199–200, 388–389
Burial
  of Jesus 74–75, 126–127, 207,

—7—

Four: Start With The Cross Reference Notes

> **Jesus Chooses the Twelve Apostles**
> *(Also Matt. 10.1–4; Luke 6.12–16)*
>
> ¹³ Then Jesus went up a hill and called to himself the men he wanted. They came to him ¹⁴ and he chose twelve, whom he named apostles. "I have chosen you to stay with me," he told them; "I will also send you out to preach, ¹⁵ and you will have authority to drive out demons." ¹⁶ These are the twelve he chose: Simon (Jesus gave him the name Peter); ¹⁷ James and his brother John, the sons of Zebedee (Jesus gave them the name Boanerges, which means "Men of Thunder"); ¹⁸ Andrew, Philip, Bartholomew, Matthew, Thomas, James the son of Alphaeus, Thaddaeus, Simon the patriot, ¹⁹ and Judas Iscariot, who became the traitor.

Each section of each book is identified by a bold print heading. Under many of these headings, especially in the Gospels, there are references in parentheses to other parts of Scripture that deal with the same or similar event, teaching, or passage.

** Whenever a passage suggests other similar passages, use the cross reference notes to find them, then read the other passages to compare similarities and differences.

** If there are three or four references to a passage in one of the Gospels, divide the class into the same number of groups. Give each group identical questions to answer from their passage. Then compare answers.

** When focusing on a passage that has several cross references, teachers can read the other passages in order to develop a greater understanding of the central concept as it appears in more than one context.

Twenty Ways to Use Line Drawings

** Introduction

** Have Fun With Them

** Organize Into Categories

** Arrange In Chronological Order

** Motivate Creative Writing

** Create Additional Line Drawings

** Use With Self-Instructional Worksheet

** Play Games

** Stimulate Memorizing

** Select Favorites

** Create Titles or Captions

** Trace For Enlargement

** Compare With Other Art

** Starter For Dramatics

** State Questions

** Tell A Story

** Copy As Slides

** Find Photos To Communicate The Same Concept

** Divide Class Into Small Groups

** Give As A Gift

** Many Other Ways

Five: Twenty Ways To Use The Line Drawings

FIRST, A WORD ABOUT THE LINE DRAWINGS

Miss Annie Vallotton is the creator of the line drawing illustrations for T.E.V. Miss Vallotton is a wonderful Swiss woman who is a remarkable teacher using her gifts of drawing, singing, story-telling, and drama to communicate so effectively when addressing a group of persons.

The experience of an evening with Annie Vallotton is one to be long-remembered by our family. After that evening in November, 1971, our daughter, Cathy (age 15 at that time), said on the way home, "If I had one wish for my children it would be that they could have Annie as their teacher of the Bible. An hour a week with her for one year and they would learn all they need to know about the Bible."
Perhaps a bit over-stated, but Cathy's comment reflects the impression persons receive after encountering Annie Vallotton.

Miss Vallotton says of her line drawings, "You will notice that many of the facial details are not completed in my drawings. It is not that I am lazy or do not know how to draw faces. Rather, I think that the face is the most expressive feature of a person and I want the reader to participate in completing the drawing by imagining his own facial expression."

Through the simplicity, beauty and honesty of her line drawings, Annie Vallotton is inviting each of us to participate with her to interpret the meaning of Scripture for ourselves. Not only is that a very generous gesture by Annie, it is also a very sound educational principle; involve the learner directly in the process of his own learning and what he perceives and receives will be valuable and lasting for his own life.

SOURCES OF THE LINE DRAWINGS

1. The basic source is in the standard publication of T.E.V. by the American Bible Society. There are 192 drawings in the complete New Testament.

   At a very reasonable cost copies can be ordered direct from the American Bible Society, and a teacher can afford to purchase three or more copies to cut up the line drawings and mount on blank 4x6 inch file cards to use in the many ways listed below. The cards in this format could also have the text typed, or cut out and mounted on the reverse side. Or, the text reference could be indicated without printing the whole text.

2. As of June, 1973, the American Bible Society has published thirty-five line drawings in color with text on reverse side. The line drawings in this format are called Scripture Cards. They are available in packages of 100 per drawing. (See Bibliography for A. B. S. address.)

3. As a service to teachers and others we (GRIGGS EDUCATIONAL SERVICE) have collated the twenty different cards in a single packet of one card each with a brief instruction paper. These packets are available from GRIGGS EDUCATIONAL SERVICE. (See Bibliography.)

4. The American Bible Society has single Gospel editions in large print that also include the line drawings. These are excellent for use with a thermofax machine in order to produce transparencies or to cut out and mount on larger cards.

5. Twelve of the line drawings have been reproduced in a poster format, 16 x 22 inches and are available from the American Bible Society. The drawings in this format include:

- The Lord's Supper
- I Will Teach You to Catch Men
- There Is No Difference
- Sing Praise to God
- The Shepherds And the Angels
- Let Us Go
- Jesus the Good Shepherd
- Love Your Fellow Man
- The Lost Son
- The Sower
- God Bless the King
- He Has Risen

WAYS TO USE LINE DRAWINGS

1. *Have Fun With Them!* With teachers in a training event I often give each group of two or three teachers a packet of thirty-five cards and suggest they spend five minutes doing whatever they want with them. After five minutes I interrupt and ask them to suggest the ways they are using them. We usually get a list of six to a dozen different ways. Then I suggest they work in larger groups (four to six persons) to brainstorm for fifteen minutes to think of ten different ways the Scripture Cards can be used in the classroom with students. Most groups come up with more than ten ways. I suggest they print their list on a sheet of newsprint or an overhead transparency that can be seen by the rest of the group. In one group of thirty-two teachers a composite list of forty-one different ways of using Scripture Cards was presented. Many of those ways are suggested in what follows.

   A pack of cards could be given to students to have fun with them without any specific instructions. It is always interesting to see what students do with them. Try it!

2. *Organize Cards Into Categories.* There are several ways to motivate students to classify the cards into various categories. Give an individual student a pack of cards or encourage students to work in pairs. The instructions could be one or more of the following:

   ** "Organize the cards into as many and whatever categories you can think of." You will be surprised by the many different categories the students discover.

   ** "Select all the cards that are associated with events or actions of Jesus' life."

Again Jesus began to teach by Lake Galilee. The crowd that gathered around him was so large that he got into a boat . . . He used parables to teach them many things.

Mark 4:1, 2

** "Put the cards in two stacks, the ones you recognize and the ones that are unfamiliar." This would be an excellent informal pre-testing technique for the teacher to use to discover what the students remember about the parts of Scripture represented by the Scripture Cards.

** "Use only feelings as headings for categories and identify as many cards as possible according to those feelings."

** The teacher could pre-select a topic and students could select as many cards as they wish to associate in some way with that topic. "Using all the cards, select any ones that in some way represent some feelings or ideas you have about Christmas." After doing this, spend some time sharing reasons why particular cards were selected.

Putting the Scripture cards in categories is an activity students of all ages and abilities can do and be successful. Such activities could be planned for students who come early or who are finished with their work earlier than others or who need a more visual kind of activity.

3. *Arrange Cards in Chronological Order.* There are enough cards in the pack related to the life of Jesus that students, after selecting all of them in that category, could arrange them in chronological order. This could be an activity for individuals or for pairs and would provide a good motivation to read the Gospels in order to see if their order is accurate. The students could compare the results of their work and possibly help each other to rearrange them in order to achieve the correct order. The difficulty of this task can be increased if the teacher has cards made directly from the line drawings in the T.E.V. For instance, in the thirty-five Scripture cards there are only four or five that relate to Jesus' last week, from Palm Sunday to Easter. However, there are more than twenty line drawings scattered among the four Gospels related to that same period. I have used packs of those twenty cards with pastors who were really challenged to place them in chronological order.

While they were eating, Jesus took the bread, gave a prayer of thanks, broke it, and gave it to his disciples. "Take it," he said, "this is my body." Then he took the cup, gave thanks to God, and handed it to them; and they all drank from it.

Mark 14:22-24

4. *Use To Motivate Creative Writing.* Students could be given a card or encouraged to select their own card as a basis for creative writing activity. There are several possible approaches to creative writing and the students could select which approach they prefer.

   ** Write a story — using the title of the card and/or the drawing students could create their own imaginative story.

   ** Write a paraphrase — focus on the Scripture text and rewrite the narrative in their own words.

   ** Write a poem — a free verse, cinquain, or haiku poem could be a beautiful response to the visual and verbal message of the card.

   ** Write a song — some students have musical talent sufficient for writing an original song.

5. *Students Can Create Their Own Line Drawings.* The line drawings are the essence of simplicity. They are not easy to draw, but they do suggest that one could make his own line drawings by using simple stick figures. There are many parts of Scripture for which line drawings have not been created. The students could create their own. Or, students could use one Scripture Card as the center picture of a five-frame story strip. They could create two drawings to represent actions or concepts *before* and two drawings to represent actions *after* the card in the middle.

6. *Line Drawings As Part of Self-Instructional Worksheet.* Many times teachers need activities and resources for students who arrive early, who are finished with their work early, or who have other special needs. Also, there are times when teachers may want to provide opportunities for students to select learning activities that they will pursue on their own or with another person. A printed, self-instructional worksheet may be one way to respond to these situations. What follows is an example on one such worksheet on the subject of Parables.

A. On the other side of this page six different parables are illustrated. Name the parables just by looking at the drawings.

   1.   4.
   2.   5.
   3.   6.

B. If you have trouble identifying any of the parables, look up the following passages of Scripture:

   Luke 10:25-37   Matthew 18:10-4   Matthew 18:21-35
   Mark 4:1-9   Luke 15:11-32   John 10:1-6

C. *Look* at each drawing and read each parable, then express in a few words, or in some other form of creative expression, the essential meanings and/or feelings that are communicated to you.

D. *Read* several more parables:

   Mark 12:1-12   Matthew 20:1-16   Mark 4:21-34

   Create your own line drawings describing one or more of these parables.

   Or, *express* one of these parables in some other creative form of your choice.

Jesus Teaches With PARABLES

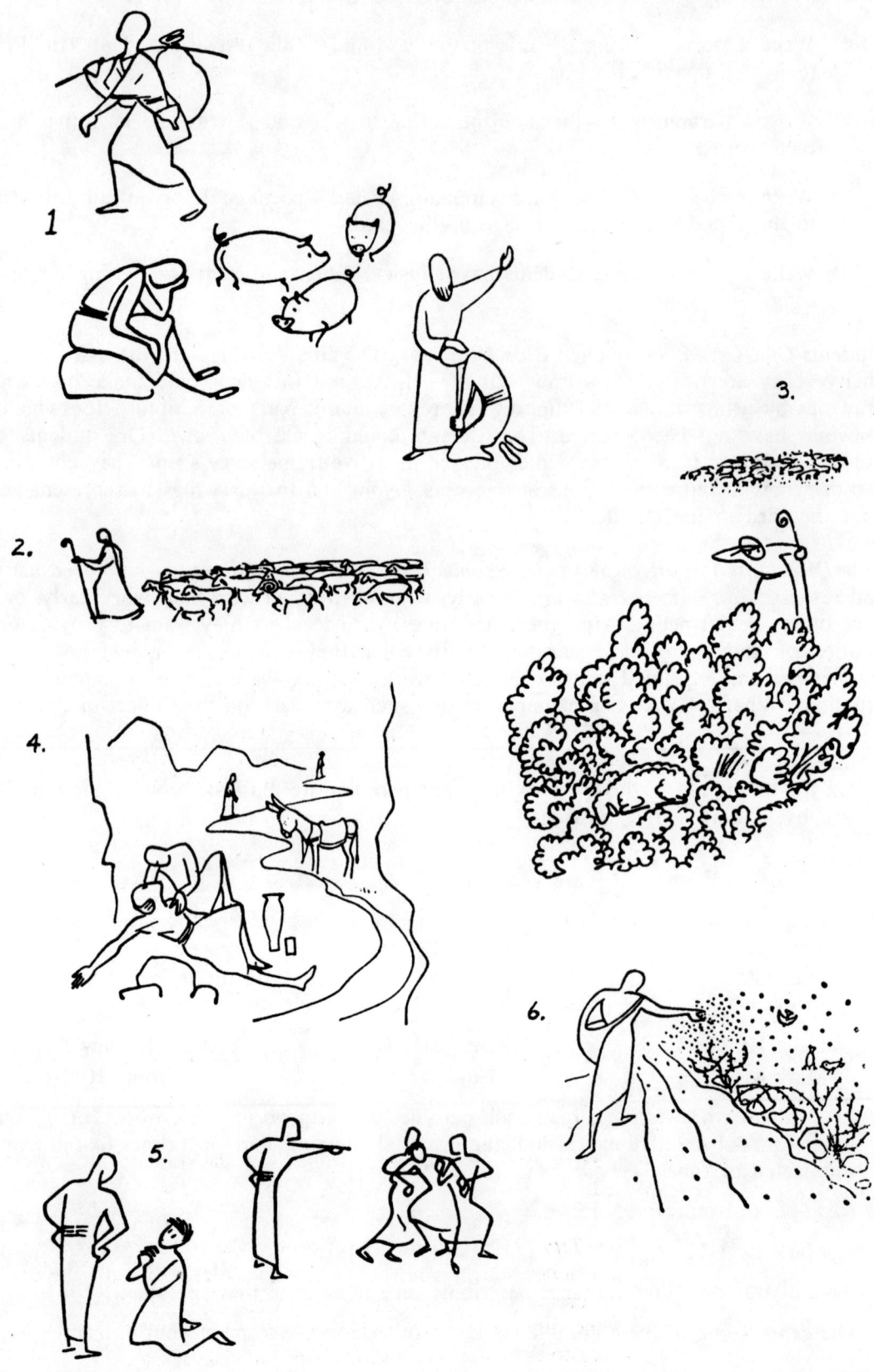

7. *Play Games With Scripture Cards.* Familiar games like Lotto, Concentration, Fish, or many others may provide models that can be used to create a game to play in the classroom using Scripture Cards.

8. *Use Cards To Stimulate Memorizing.* Even though memorization is not the most significant learning activity there may be times when teachers want to be sure that students remember particular parts of Scripture. The Scripture Cards can provide a fun way to motivate students to memorize the passages associated with the cards.

But a certain Samaritan who was traveling that way came upon him, and when he saw the man his heart was filled with pity. He went over to him, poured oil and wine on his wounds and bandaged them; then he put the man on his own animal and took him to an inn, where he took care of him.

Luke 10:33, 34

9. *Select Your Favorite Scripture Card.* Many persons very naturally select cards that they like better than others. A good activity for introducing the cards for the first time is to instruct persons to select one card that is their favorite. After they select their favorite card they could . . .

   . . . share their favorite with several other persons to discuss why they chose the ones they chose;

   . . . find someone who selected the same card to share together their reasons for making the choice;

   . . . compare their card with others until another person's card is similar in meaning or feeling to their card;

   . . . team up with another person or two to combine their cards to communicate one message;

   . . . draw themselves into the line drawing of the card.

   If the teacher has enough extra cards, it may be possible to let the students keep their favorite cards that they selected.

10. *Students Create Their Own Titles or Captions.* The Scripture Cards have titles already printed on them. However, the teacher or students could cover the titles with small pieces of colored tape. Then they could create their own titles or captions. If the line drawings were cut from the pages of T.E.V. and mounted on 4 x 6 inch cards, then students could write directly on the cards. It would be possible for the teacher to select some specific line drawings and

have them duplicated by mimeograph or spirit duplicator for the students to write on without ruining a prepared card.

11. *Trace To Make An Enlargement.* By use of an overhead projector, poster board, and felt-tip pens, it is possible to create enlargements of the line drawings to use as posters or banners. First it is necessary to trace a line drawing from a Scripture Card on the overhead projector to project on a piece of poster paper instead of a screen. The size of the projected image can be adjusted by moving the projector closer to or away from the poster paper. When the right size is determined, use felt-tip marker to trace around the lines of the projected image. The finished product is a poster size line drawing which could be used as a pattern for a banner or as the basis for a poster or teaching picture.

12. *Compare With Other Works of Art.* Many of the line drawings are of familiar passages that have been subjects for many artistic expressions through the centuries. It would be an interesting experience to mount photos or prints of several artists' interpretations of a passage of Scripture for which there is also a Scripture Card. There may be some value to adding a couple of the more traditional teaching pictures to the display.

The teacher could guide the class in a discussion that may begin with questions such as:

** Which of the paintings or drawings is your favorite? Why?

** What do you think the artist was trying to communicate through his painting?

** What feeings are communicated to you through each of the paintings?

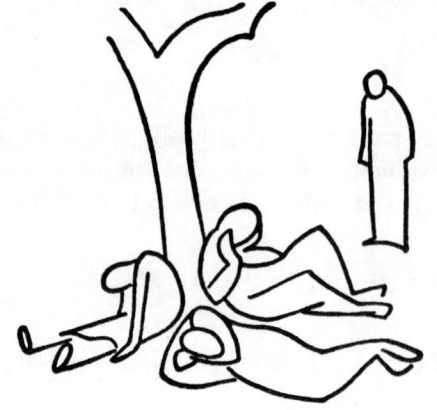

Then he returned and found the three disciples asleep, and said to Peter, "Simon, are you asleep? Weren't you able to stay awake for one hour?"

Mark 14:37

13. *Use As Starter for Informal Dramatics.* Scripture Cards could be used in a variety of ways to enhance the dramatic skills and interests of the students.

** Students could be divided into two teams to *play charades* or *pantomime*. Give each team a different selection of cards. Members of each team take turns charading or pantomiming the message of the card to see if the other team can guess what they are doing. If students have become so familiar with the sets of thirty-five cards, then the difficulty could be increased by using other line drawings from the text of T.E.V. Cut out and mount them on 4 x 6 inch cards.

** Many of the Scripture Cards represent events in the lives of Jesus and the disciples. These cards could be used as a basis for developing a *creative drama* to express the action, feeling, and message of the events.

** Just by looking at the drawing on a Scripture Card it is possible to imagine a situation of conflict, decision-making, or personal encounter. Students could identify with the situation in their own creative way and with one or more other persons develop a *role play* of the situation.

14. *What Questions Do You Have?* Teachers could select one or more Scripture Cards to use for motivating students to state their own questions. If one Scripture Card is used, the students could be given several minutes to look at the line drawing and read the text on the other side. After this brief time each student could be instructed to write down or think about one or two questions that come to his mind after looking at and reading the card. When students have time to think and write their questions, the teacher could encourage them to state their questions and copy them down on a chalk board, newsprint, or overhead transparency. As we have stated before, students are much more motivated to pursue their own questions than they are the teacher's questions.

15. *Tell A Story With a Series of Drawings and/or Captions.* Give pairs of students identical sets of cards and instruct them to use the line drawings separately, the captions separately, or both together to create a story or message. It is really interesting to see the variety of stories and messages that are created by different groups even though they all start with identical cards. An example of a story that was created by one pair of older students using titles from ten different cards:

> "Follow me . . . I will teach you to catch men . . .
> What shall we do? . . . Love your fellow man . . .
> There is no difference . . . The Son of God . . .
> A light for my path . . . He makes me glad . . .
> Let us go . . . In all this world."

16. *Copy As Slides To Use For Worship.* Using a single lens reflex camera, with close-up capability, it is possible to make slides of the Scripture Cards. When projected on the screen in a darkened room the line drawings are very vivid and beautiful. Such slides could be projected during the reading of Scripture, during a time of meditation, or as an illustration for a sermon. The slides could also be used by students in the classroom in several creative ways:

   - to write and record their own script to accompany the slides;

   - to arrange in chronological order;

   - to use as visual interpretations of words in a song or hymn;

   - as focus for a worship setting.

The Spirit is the guarantee that we shall receive what God has promised his people, and assures us that God will give complete freedom to those who are his. Let us praise his glory!

Ephesians 1:14

17. *Find Photos To Communicate the Same Concept.* Start with a large piece of construction paper, butcher paper or space on a bulletin board. Select one Scripture Card as the focus for the activity. Work individually or in small groups. Use a box of old magazines with lots of photos. Place the Scripture Cards in the center of the space, then select, cut out, and mount photographs, headlines, advertisements, cartoons, etc., that emphasize the same concept or feeling as the original Scripture Card. The end product will be a beautiful montage communicating one key concept.

18. *Use To Divide Class Into Small Groups.* Starting with several sets of Scripture Cards, the teacher could pre-select two, three or four different cards. Put the selected cards from all sets into one stack, shuffle them, and when students come to class, let each one select a card. Later in the class the students could be divided into small groups according to the cards they selected as they arrived.

19. *Give Scripture Cards As A Gift.* Scripture Cards in complete sets or individually make wonderful gifts for family, friends, shut-ins, absentee students, persons traveling, and others.

20. *Many Other Ways . . .* This chapter is in danger of becoming long enough to become a book of its own. Instead of writing descriptions of additional ways to use Scripture Cards I will just identify them by descriptive titles. The reader can interpret each title in his own way and with his creative spirit can do with it what he wants.

- ** Make a hanging mobile.
- ** Focus on the feelings in each drawing.
- ** Use as an ice-breaker in large groups.
- ** Mount as a display on bulletin board.
- ** Use in worship for unison reading.
- ** Use in worship to focus silent meditation.
- ** Card game to match Scripture with drawing.
- ** Give cards to students when they learn the story.
- ** Which person in the drawing would you like to be? Why?
- ** Students draw themselves and place in the line drawing.
- ** Use for woodblock, linoleum print, embroidery, or stitchery.
- ** Find the Scripture associated with specific drawings.
- ** Combine with Cinquain or Haiku poems.
- ** Have cards available for "free-time" activities.
- ** Create a tableau of the same event.
- ** Write a song or select songs to express message of the card.
- ** Use to decorate the room.
- ** Have fun with them, create your own ways of using them.

Suddenly a great army of heaven's angels appeared with the angel, singing praises to God, "Glory to God in the highest heaven, and peace on earth to those with whom he is pleased!"

Luke 2:13, 14

Focus On One Gospel

Four Teaching Activities

** Read From Beginning to the End

** Select A Key Subject

** Make A List of Your Own Questions

** Identify the Important Actions of Jesus

So Jesus said to the twelve disciples, "And you — would you like to leave also?" Simon Peter answered him: "Lord, to whom would we go? You have the words that give eternal life. And now we believe and know that you are the Holy One from God."

John 6:67-69

Six: Focus On One Gospel

In studying and teaching the Bible, persons usually do it in "bits and pieces." Seldom do persons gain a sense of the wholeness of the Bible or even one book of the Bible. For students of all ages from older elementary through adult I think that it is important to provide learning experiences where they do experience the wholeness of the Bible.

To illustrate a variety of ways to focus on one Book of the Bible we are going to work with the Gospel of Mark. What we do with the Gospel of Mark could be done with any or all of the other three Gospels. The same principles and strategies could be adapted and applied to other books in the Old and New Testaments.

"Listen! There was a man who went out to sow. As he scattered the seed in the field, some of it fell along the path, and the birds came and ate it up. Some of it fell on rocky ground, where there was little soil. The seeds soon sprouted, because the soil wasn't deep. Then when the sun came up it burned the young plants, and because the roots had not grown deep enough the plants soon dried up. Some of the seed fell among thorns, which grew up and choked the plants, and they didn't bear grain. But some good seeds fell in good soil, and the plants sprouted, grew, and bore grain: some had thirty grains, others sixty, and others one hundred." And Jesus concluded, "Listen, then, if you have ears to hear with."

Mark 4:3-8

READ FROM BEGINNING TO END

One way to read the Gospel of Mark is to read it as you would any other book, from the first to last chapters. In this way a person will get an overview of the Gospel and no doubt there would be some parts that would be more memorable than others. However, the truths and values of Scripture cannot be fully appreciated and comprehended in one reading. The Bible is a very special book containing the thoughts, feelings, beliefs, and interpretations of many persons. The Bible is the Word of God. God, through the power and presence of his Spirit in the lives of persons, has been able to communicate what it means to "love God with one's whole being and to love others as oneself." Because of the unending values of the Word of God through the words of men it is necessary to read the Bible over and over again so that persons may grow in their faith and love for God and man.

Even though reading from first to last chapters is a valid way to read the Gospel of Mark there are several other ways to approach the reading of Mark which may increase the value and effectiveness of one's study.

SELECT A KEY SUBJECT

The Gospels themselves are brief summaries of three years in the life of Jesus and his followers. There are lots of persons, events, and concepts that are central to each Gospel. One way to read a Gospel is to select beforehand one subject to provide a focus for reading.

Early in the morning the chief priests met hurriedly with the elders, the teachers of the Law, and the whole Council, and made their plans. They put Jesus in chains, took him away, and handed him over to Pilate. Pilate questioned him, "Are you the king of the Jews?" Jesus answered, "So you say."

Mark 15:1, 2

Read the Gospel of Mark and look for one subject at a time.

** Look for all the *parables of Jesus* . . . make a list of them . . . categorize them by subject . . . select several to study in depth.

** Look for all the words that are used as *titles or descriptions of Jesus* . . . write them all down . . . note the number of times each is used . . . paraphrase the titles or descriptions in your own words . . . look for the same titles or descriptions in other Gospels . . . what new titles and descriptions do you find in other Gospels . . . summarize your own insights and impressions.

When they arrived in Jerusalem, Jesus went to the temple and began to drive out all those who bought and sold in the temple. . . .He then taught the people, "It is written in the Scriptures that God said, 'My house will be called a house of prayer for all peoples.' But you have turned it into a hideout for thieves!"

Mark 11:15, 17

—21—

Some of the titles and descriptions I found in the first eight chapters of Mark include:

- Son of God
- Jesus of Nazareth
- God's holy messenger
- Son of Man
- Teacher
- Prophet
- Messiah

** Look for all *the oppositions to Jesus* categorize them according to personal, political and religious oppositions . . . what caused the opposition . . . what was the result of the opposition . . . how did Jesus respond to the opposition?

** Look for all the *encounters between Jesus and his disciples* . . . how does Jesus treat the disciples . . . how do the disciples respond to Jesus . . . what are the places and circumstances of the encounters?

** Look for all the *miracles of Jesus* . . . make a list of them . . . what are the similarities and differences between them . . . what is the reason for Jesus performing the miracle . . . what happens after the miracle?

The above are just examples of the types of subjects to look for in order to focus one's reading of the Gospel of Mark or one of the other Gospels. This is an activity that can be done by an individual person to guide his own reading. A teacher could use a similar approach to guide the study of the whole class.

MAKE A LIST OF YOUR OWN QUESTIONS

Persons could read a Gospel and write a list of questions that come to mind in the process of doing the reading. This would be an especially appropriate activity for teachers to do for themselves in preparation for teaching a particular Gospel.

After making a list of questions that the person wants to pursue further, then time should be spent using a Bible Commentary, Bible Dictionary, and Bible Atlas to search for answers to the questions.

This activity could also be used in an introductory session with students who were beginning study of a Gospel.

IDENTIFY THE IMPORTANT ACTIONS OF JESUS

This activity is appropriate for a whole class or individual persons. The process is written in the form of instructions to the students. Each student needs a copy of T.E.V. and is assigned or chooses one chapter of the Gospel of Mark to be his responsibility.

- "In your chapter look for all of the important actions of Jesus. Write them down on a sheet of paper." (In some chapters there may be no actions of Jesus depending upon the Gospel that is selected. In the Gospel of Mark there is at least one thing that Jesus does or that happens to him in each of the sixteen chapters.)

- "Look over your list of actions of Jesus and select one or two actions that you think are the most important or representative ones." (If there are fewer than sixteen students, assign the next chapter to the one who completes his work first. If there are more than sixteen students, encourage some of them to work in pairs.)

- "Now that you all have selected one or two important actions of Jesus from your chapter let's list them." (Write them down in order from chapter one to sixteen. Write on chalk-board, newsprint, or overhead transparency.)

- "That is a good list of thirty or more actions of Jesus. Look at the whole list. Select what you think are the top-ten most important actions. Use any criteria you want to determine what you think are the top-ten actions of Jesus."

- "Now rank your top-ten choices in the order of highest priority to lowest. Write them down with the highest as No. 1 and the lowest as No. 10.

This could be the last step of the activity to be followed by a period of comparing and discussing among all the students. Or, one more step could be taken. Organize students in groups of three to five persons to compare their choices and ranking of the top-ten actions of Jesus. After a few minutes of comparing and discussing in the small groups, the students could then be instructed to work as a group to come to a concensus of the top-five actions of Jesus and rank them in order of priority also.

Then Jesus took the five loaves and the two fish, looked up to heaven, and gave thanks to God. He broke the loaves and gave them to his disciples to distribute to the people. He also divided the two fish among them all. Everyone ate and had enough.

Mark 6:41, 42

What follows is what one particular class and student did in completing the above instructions as they worked with the Gospel of Mark.

A. *The important actions of Jesus in each chapter of the Gospel of Mark.*

JESUS . . . .

1:9	- is baptized
1:14	- calls four fishermen
1:21	- conquers an evil spirit
1:40	- makes a leper clean
2:1	- heals a paralyzed man
2:18	- answers questions about fasting
3:1	- heals a man on the Sabbath
3:13	- chooses twelve disciples
4:1	- teaches with parables
4:35	- calms a storm
5:1	- heals a man with evil spirits
5:21	- heals Jairus' daughter
6:1	- is rejected in Nazareth
6:6	- sends out the twelve disciples

6:30 - feeds 5000 people
6:45 - walks on the water
7:1 - responds to the Pharisees' questions
8:11 - does not perform a miracle for Pharisees
8:22 - heals a blind man
8:31 - speaks about his suffering and death
9:33 - responds to the question, "Who is the greatest?"
10:13 - blesses the little children
10:17 - calls a rich young man to follow him
10:46 - heals blind Bartimaeus
11:1 - triumphant entry into Jerusalem
11:15 - cleanses the temple of the money changers
12:28 - answers the question, "Which is the greatest Commandment?"
12:41 - responds to the widow's offering
13:1 - speaks about destruction of the temple
14:12 - eats his last meal with the disciples
14:27 - predicts Peter's denial
14:32 - prays in Gethsemene
14:43 - arrested in the garden
14:53 - appears before the council
15:6 - sentenced to death
15:33 - is crucified and dies
16:1 - risen from the dead

Some women were there, looking on from a distance. Among them were Mary Magdalene, Mary the mother of the younger James and of Joses, and Salome. They had followed Jesus while he was in Galilee and helped him. Many other women were there also, who had come to Jerusalem with him.

Mark 15:40, 41

B. *The ten most important actions of Jesus are:* (As selected by one student.)

(2)   1:9   Jesus is baptized
(5)   3:1   Jesus heals a man on the Sabbath
(3)   3:13   Jesus chooses twelve disciples
(7)   4:1   Jesus teaches with parables
(8)   6:6   Jesus sends out the twelve disciples
(10) 10:13 Jesus blesses the little children
(4)   11:1   Jesus' triumphant entry into Jerusalem
(6)   12:28 Jesus answers questions about greatest Commandment
(9)   14:12 Jesus eats his last meal with his disciples
(1)   16:1   Jesus risen from the dead

C. *That student ranked the above ten events as noted by the numbers in parentheses in the left column.*

So they went out and ran from the grave, because fear and terror were upon them. They said nothing to anyone, because they were afraid.

Mark 16:8

This activity of identifying, selecting, and ranking important actions of Jesus in one of the Gospels may take more than one class session. It is the kind of activity that could be done successfully with students from fifth grade and older. It has worked very well in classes with mixed age groups; adults, youth and children all working together. It is also an activity that a family could do together at home, or on a vacation camping trip.

There are several teaching-learning principles that should be recognized when using this activity:

- ** It is possible to provide an overview of a large body of material (a whole Gospel) in a relatively short period of time.

- ** Individual students are responsible for a small amount of material (one chapter) which they can read in depth.

- ** What each student does is very important for the successful participation of the entire class.

- ** The process of identifying all the actions of Jesus then selecting one or two most important actions is helpful to students as they are encouraged to reflect, compare and make choices. This leads to a high level of motivation and involvement.

- ** Persons tend to read a Gospel and consider all parts of it as equal in value. That may be true in terms of the Gospel being a part of the Word of God, but on the other hand, all events in Jesus' life are not equal. Many events have gone unrecorded because those who experienced Jesus and wrote about him were themselves selective of what was most important. The students can participate in the same process through the activity described above.

- ** When students read one or more chapters looking for something specific, such as the actions of Jesus, then they know there is a purpose for their reading. Often we ask students to read something without giving them any reasons for doing the reading.

- ** Teachers should resist moralizing and imposing their own values on the students. Hopefully, teachers will have made their own choices about the most important events in Jesus' life, but that does not give license to impose those choices upon the students. It is much more helpful to the students and they will be much more motivated if they can participate freely in making their own choices.

- ** Perhaps the most important part of the whole activity is the period of discussion and reflection that happens at the end of the session. Some questions to consider using could include:

- When you look at the summary of all the important events of Jesus that we have listed, what observations or insights do you have?

- What criteria did you use in selecting the ten most important events?

- Why did you select your top most important event as number one?

- If you were to write your own Gospel using only the top-ten events of Jesus' life, what would be communicated about Jesus?

A very strong wind blew up and the waves began to spill over into the boat, so that it was about to fill with water. Jesus was in the back of the boat, sleeping with his head on a pillow. The disciples woke him up and said, "Teacher, don't you care that we are about to die?" Jesus got up and commanded the wind, "Be quiet!" and said to the waves, "Be still!" The wind died down, and there was a great calm.

Then Jesus said to his disciples, "Why are you frightened? Are you still without faith?"

Mark 4:37-40

Focus On the Acts of the Apostles

- ** Define the Word Disciple

- ** The Twelve Apostles

- ** The Twelfth Apostle

- ** Pentecost - The Church's Birthday

- ** Some Key Persons in the Book of Acts

- ** The Message of the Apostles

- ** Map Study

- ** Some Important Meetings in Jerusalem

- ** What Do We Do Now?

Many of them believed his message and were baptized; about three thousand people were added to the group that day. They spent their time in learning from the apostles, taking part in the fellowship, and sharing in the fellowship meals and the prayers.

Acts 2:41, 42

Seven: Focus On The Acts Of The Apostles

What follows is a series of activities that teachers could use with students to guide them in a study of the book of *The Acts of the Apostles*. Depending upon the ages of the students, the length of the class period and the resources available, some or all of these activities could be used with the students. It will work best if teachers will be selective of the activities they deem most appropriate and then take from and add to these activities to adapt them to their own classes.

ACTIVITY ONE: DEFINE THE WORD "DISCIPLE"

OBJECTIVE

At the end of the session the students should be able to explain in their own words what the word "disciple" meant in Jesus' day and what it means today.

PROCESS

After providing each student with a copy of T.E.V. of the New Testament the following steps can be taken: (The steps are stated as instructions to the students.)

- "Find the word 'disciple' in the Word List in the back of the book."

- "Read the definition of 'disciple' and decide on one or more questions that come to mind."

- "Let's make a list of our questions. You state the question you have in mind and I will write it down." (Reread Chapter Two for some guidelines related to this activity.)

- "Now that we have a good list of questions, let's spend the next ten to fifteen minutes searching for answers. You can use any of the resources on the table. (*People of the Bible, Bible Encyclopedia, Concise Concordance* and Index in the T.E.V. and/or others.) Start with any questions you choose and see what answers you can find. You can work on as many questions as you have time and interest."

- "With all the good searching you have done you should have found some interesting information and ideas that will help us answer the questions we started with. Let's share what we have found."

With time for sharing and discussion, this activity should take between twenty and thirty minutes.

ACTIVITY TWO: THE TWELVE APOSTLES

OBJECTIVE

At the end of the session the students should be able to find the list of the twelve apostles in three different places in the New Testament and name nine of the twelve apostles.

One of the twelve disciples, Thomas (called the Twin), was not with them when Jesus came. So the other disciples told him, "We saw the Lord!" Thomas said to them, "If I do not see the scars of the nails in his hands, and put my fingers on those scars, and my hand in his side, I will not believe."

A week later the disciples were together indoors again, and Thomas was with them. The doors were locked, but Jesus came and stood among them and said, "Peace be with you." Then he said to Thomas, "Put your finger here, and look at my hands; then stretch out your hand and put it in my side. Stop your doubting, and believe!" Thomas answered him, "My Lord and my God!" Jesus said to him, "Do you believe because you see me? How happy are those who believe without seeing me!"

John 20:24-29

PROCESS (Steps are stated as instructions to the students.)

- "Using the Index in T.E.V., find at least one listing of the twelve apostles in the Gospels."

    Allow time for searching. When several students have found one of the listings, have the whole class turn to that passage. The lists will be found in: Matthew 10:1-4, Mark 3:13-19, and Luke 6:12-16.

- "Notice under the heading of 'The Twelve Apostles' there are two other passages of Scripture identified where you will find the twelve apostles listed again. Read all three passages. Compare the names in each list. Make two observations about the three lists:

    1. What are the similarities of the three lists?

    2. What are the differences between the three lists?

    Read the lists carefully and work in small groups to make your observations."

    Allow sufficient time for the students to read and compare the three lists and to make their observations about the similarities and differences. Then compare observations by discussing what they have discovered.

- "Using the *Concise Concordance* (Proper names are listed separately in the back.) and the Index in T.E.V., look up some of the names of the Apostles."

- Based on what you have discovered about the three lists and what you noticed in the Concordance and Index, which of the Apostles are you likely to find the most information about?"

- "Select the name of one apostle on which to do some further research. Use the available resources (*People of the Bible, Young Readers' Book of Bible Stories, Golden Bible Atlas, R.S.V. Concise Concordance,* and *T.E.V. Index*) to search for information about your person."

- "As you are reading, consider the following questions:

    What does the apostle's name mean?
    How did the apostle first encounter Jesus?
    What special things did the apostle do?
    What kind of relationship did the apostle have with Jesus?
    What kind of person was the apostle?
    What influence did the apostle have on the early Church?

- "After you have found enough information about your apostle, summarize what you know by writing or dictating a letter as if it were a letter of introduction to someone else. You could start the letter by saying: "To Whom It May Concern. It is my pleasure to introduce the apostle, _____. There are some things I would like to share with you about _____ . . .""

Students should then have opportunity to share their letters with others in the class. With time spent on introduction, instructions, research, summarizing, letter-writing and sharing, this activity should take between thirty and forty minutes.

ACTIVITY THREE: THE TWELFTH APOSTLE

OBJECTIVE

At the end of the session the students should be able to identify with the situation of the early apostles when they were faced with selecting a successor to Judas and to write in their own words a "job description" for an apostle.

PROCESS

The teacher could begin by leading a brief introductory discussion that would cover the following subjects:

Who were the original twelve apostles?.. What is an apostle?.. What happened to Judas? Why?.. Why would the remaining eleven apostles want to have someone to take Judas' place?

The remainder of the activity could be done by each student individually, or perhaps in groups of two or three by using the following worksheet:

Qualifications For Disciples of Jesus

We have been followers of Jesus for three years. We have had many experiences living, working, praying, traveling, and learning with Jesus. We have lived through those terrible days of Jesus' crucifixion. And, we have just recently been surprised and inspired by his renewed presence with us. Some of Jesus' last words are still ringing in our ears:

"Go, then, to all peoples everywhere and make them my disciples... You will be filled with power when the Holy Spirit comes on you and you will be witnesses for me in Jerusalem, in all of Judea and Samaria, and to the ends of the earth."

Today we are meeting to decide who will take Judas' place in the company of disciples. In order to be sure the right person is chosen we need to do two things:

First, write a brief "job description" of what a disciple can expect to do as a follower of Jesus. Second, write a brief list of the personal characteristics that should be present in a person who would be a disciple.

Disciple Job Description:

Characteristics To Look For In a Disciple:

This activity, with time for sharing and discussion could take fifteen to twenty-five minutes.

ACTIVITY FOUR: PENTECOST — THE CHURCH'S BIRTHDAY

OBJECTIVE

At the end of the session the students should be able to express in a creative form their own interpretation of Pentecost and the two central symbols of fire and wind.

Then Peter stood up with the other eleven apostles, and in a loud voice began to speak to the crowd, "Fellow Jews, and all of you who live in Jerusalem, listen to me and let me tell you what this means."

Acts 2:14

PROCESS

- Pentecost is the one Christian high holy day which has not been corrupted by commercial interests. Yet, in many churches Pentecost is hardly recognized and seldom really celebrated. The following lesson plan suggests a way of celebrating Pentecost.

- Ask the class to list in chronological order the major days of celebration in the Church. Start with Advent, then list Christmas, Ash Wednesday, Maundy Thursday, Good Friday, Easter and Pentecost. Probably the class will suggest Thanksgiving or some other national holidays. Use this as an opportunity to discuss briefly the differences. Also, it would not be surprising if they did not think of Pentecost. Focus on Pentecost. What does the name mean? Look up the word in a dictionary. Explain the biblical origin and meaning of Pentecost to the Hebrews and afterwards to the Christians. Then read Acts 2:1-15 and 37-47. (Teachers will be helped by looking up Pentecost in the *Interpreter's Dictionary of the Bible*.)

- If available, show filmstrip *The Fire and the Wind* produced by John and Mary Harrell and available from them at P.O. Box 9006, Berkeley, CA 94719. This filmstrip provides a very creative and contemporary approach to understanding Pentecost. This filmstrip is appropriate for older students. On the reverse side of the recorded script are many songs and hymns appropriate to Pentecost. One that many of the students know is "Blowin' In the Wind."

- After seeing the filmstrip play the recordings of several songs including "Blowin' In the Wind." Then ask the class, "What connection do you see between the biblical account of Pentecost and the song 'Blowin' In the Wind'?"

- The symbols of wind and fire are key to understanding Pentecost. Have one group look up passages of Scripture and Bible Dictionary sections on "wind" and another group look up "fire" in order to appreciate the significance of these two symbols for representing the presence of God's spirit in the midst of the people. Use a Bible Concordance to locate passages where the words "wind" and "spirit" are used to represent God's presence or power.

- Discuss the following questions:

    1. Where is God's Spirit at work in the world today?
    2. Where are some places where God's Spirit is needed?
    3. How do we know when God's Spirit is present?

- Have the class or group respond to the theme of Pentecost in one of several creative forms.

    1. *Montage*: With pictures, words and letters cut from magazines, create a design or statement in response to the incomplete phrase, "God's Spirit is . . . ."

    2. *Finger Painting*: With "spirit-filled" music the class can respond creatively with finger painting.

    3. *Chalk and Water Colors*: With an oil based chalk students can create a design or picture and then use water color to paint over the chalk in a variety of colors and textures.

- The thinking and creating are the most important parts of the lesson. However, much can be gained in understanding and appreciation if the students will discuss their work with the others in the class in order to share their ideas and feelings about Pentecost. This sharing could be included as a part of a brief liturgy of celebration emphasizing the power and presence of God's Spirit in the midst of us.

ACTIVITY FIVE: SOME KEY PERSONS IN THE BOOK OF ACTS

OBJECTIVE

At the end of the session the students should be able to identify by name at least five key persons in Acts and describe in their own words some characteristics and activities of each.

PROCESS

This activity is similar to part of Activity Two on the Twelve Apostles. The activity could be accomplished by using the worksheet below.

Some Key Persons In The Book of Acts

Peter — John — Stephen — Paul — James
Barnabas — John Mark — Silas — Timothy

Instructions

1. Select one person to study and think about.

2. Use resources available to answer the following questions:
    - What are some of the main actions of _____?
    - What problems or conflicts did _____ encounter?
    - What did _____ believe about Jesus?

3. Write a brief letter of recommendation for your person requesting that he be considered to be the spokesman for Jesus Christ in a debate.

- or -

Write a letter in the first person (as the person of your choice) to introduce yourself to a stranger who has written to you asking questions about Jesus Christ.

4. In whichever of the two activities you choose, be sure to include some statements of what the person believed about Jesus.

On his way to Damascus, as he came near the city, suddenly a light from the sky flashed around him. He fell to the ground and heard a voice saying to him, "Saul, Saul! Why do you persecute me?" "Who are you, Lord?" he asked. "I am Jesus, whom you persecute," the voice said. "But get up and go into the city, where you will be told what you must do."

Acts 9:3-6

ACTIVITY SIX: THE MESSAGE OF THE APOSTLES

OBJECTIVE

At the end of the session the students should be able to identify some of the major speeches or sermons in the Book of Acts and summarize in their own words the essence of the message of the apostles.

PROCESS

In the Book of Acts there are many speeches, sermons, or reports by the apostles and others. By reading these statements we can learn much about what was important to the leaders of the early Church.

The students could themselves spend time searching in Acts for passages that can be identified as a speech, sermon, or report. After making a list of all the passages they could work individually or in small groups as suggested below.

To save time the teacher may want to offer a list of passages for the students to use. Listed below are references to seven of the major speeches and sermons.

    Acts   2:14-47 . . . . Peter's sermon at Pentecost
            3:12-26 . . . . Peter's sermon in the Temple
            4:1-22   . . . . Peter and John before the Council
            7:1-53   . . . . Stephen's speech
            10:34-43 . . . . Peter's speech at Caesarea
            13:16-47 . . . . Paul's speech in the Synagogue
            26:1-29 . . . . Paul's speech before King Agrippa

(There are others that the teacher could include.)

Students could be given the following instructions:

- "Select one passage of Scripture to study further."

- "There are some things to look for while you are reading the sermon or speech —

To whom is the person speaking? Why?

What does the person believe -

- about God?

- about Jesus' life and teachings?

- about Jesus' death and resurrection?

- that his listeners should do?

What happens after the speech is delivered?

What are the reactions of the listeners?

- "After reading the speech and reflecting on the above questions, write a brief statement of belief based on what the person says."

- "If you had been the one making the speech what might you have said?"

ACTIVITY SEVEN: MAP STUDY

Map study could be included as part of other sessions in the study of Acts or a session could be devoted to using the maps to do one or more of the following activities:

1. Trace the map on an overhead projection transparency for the teacher to use as a reference point.

2. Use printed map and thermal transparency with a thermal copy machine to reproduce one or more acetate maps for teacher or students to use.

3. Use printed map or spirit master to trace or use with thermal copier to reproduce enough copies for each student to have one or more maps.

4. Locate all principle cities and bodies of water mentioned in the Book of Acts.

5. Locate the cities of each of Paul's four missionary journeys and diagram each journey on a different map.

6. Show on the map the direction and extent of the expansion of the Christian Church in the first century.

7. Make an enlargement of map to mount on bulletin board for whole class to see.

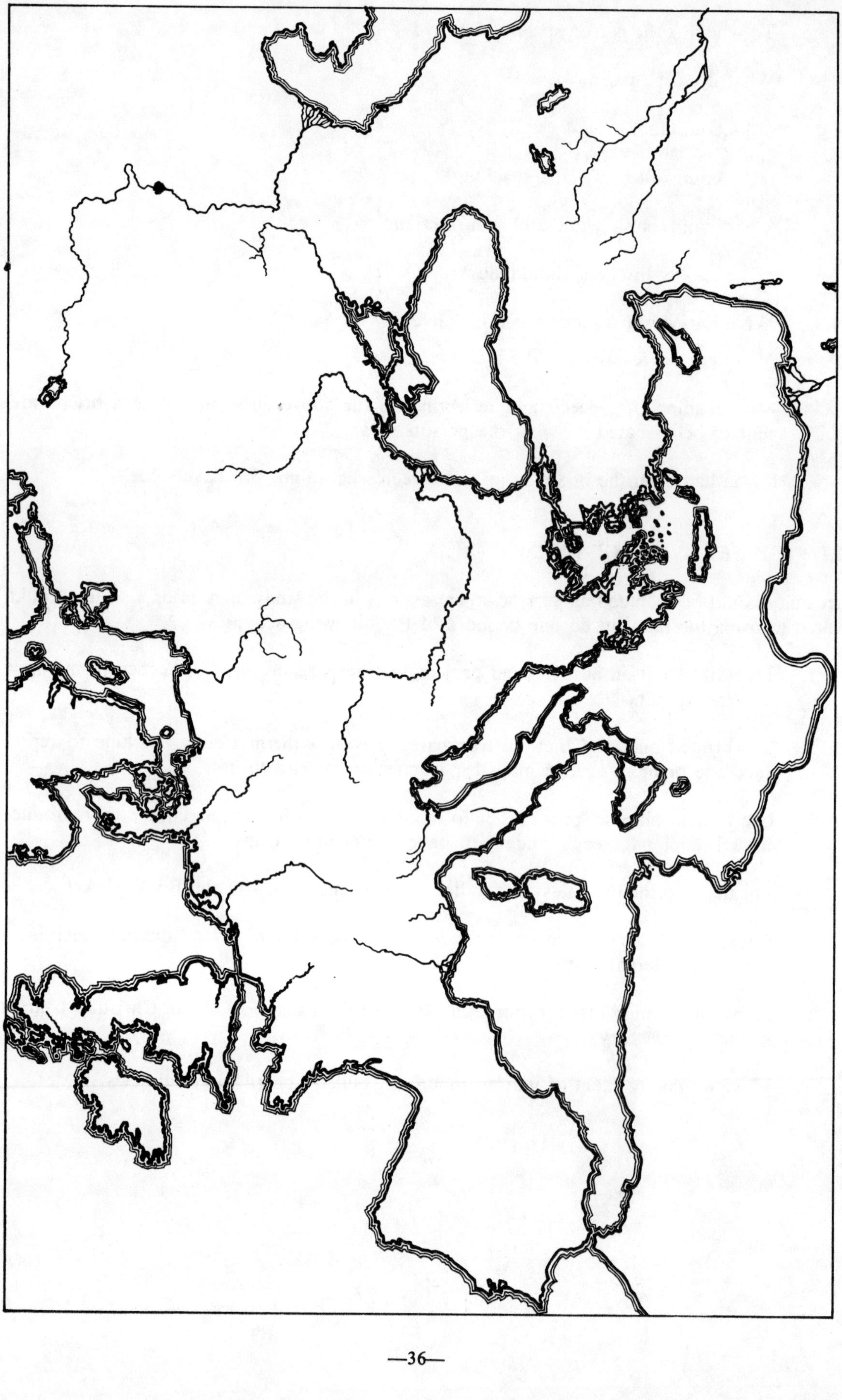

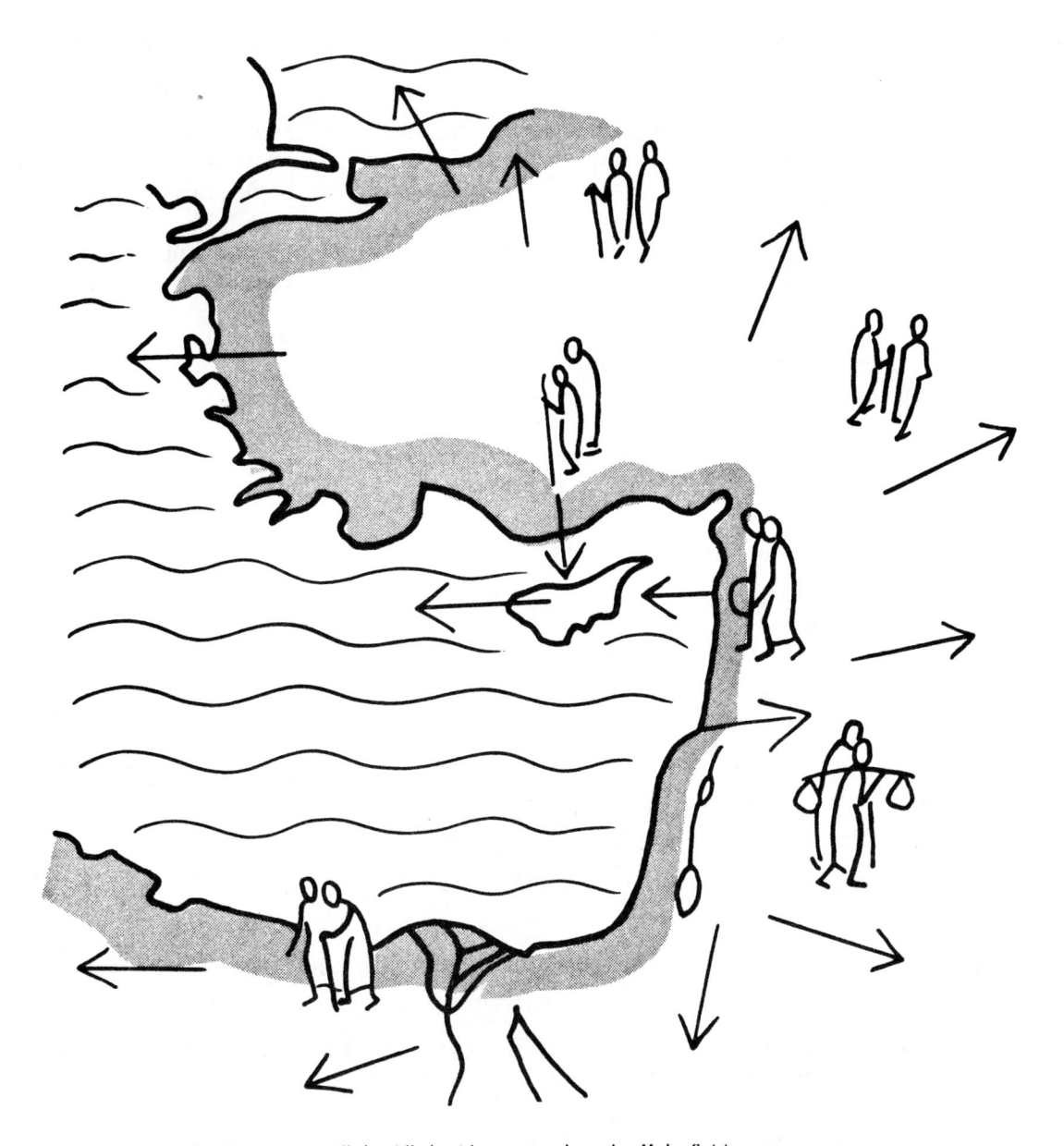

"... you will be filled with power when the Holy Spirit comes on you, and you will be witnesses for me in Jerusalem, in all of Judea and Samaria, and to the ends of the earth."

Acts 1:8

ACTIVITY EIGHT: SOME IMPORTANT MEETINGS IN JERUSALEM

OBJECTIVE

At the end of the session the students should be able to locate several of the meetings that happened in Jerusalem that are recorded in Acts and identify with the persons and circumstances of one of those meetings.

PROCESS

When reading the Book of Acts one discovers that on several occasions there were important "meetings" that were held in Jerusalem. There are similarities about these meetings as well as some significant differences. At each of the meetings important issues were dealt with and resolved. By reading about and reflecting upon these meetings it is possible to discover some of the important concerns of the early Church.

The students could themselves spend time searching in Acts for passages that describe the events and issues related to the several meetings that occurred in Jerusalem. After identifying these meetings they could work individually or in small groups as suggested below.

To save time the teacher may want to present the passages for the student to use. Listed below are references to six important meetings that happened in Jerusalem.

>   Acts   1:12-26 . . . . choosing an apostle to take Judas' place.
>   2:1-12 . . . . receiving the Holy Spirit at Pentecost.
>   9:26-31 . . . . Paul's first meeting with the Church elders.
>   11:1-8 . . . . Peter's report to the Church.
>   15:1-21 . . . . the first council of Jerusalem.
>   21:17-40 . . . . Paul returns to Jerusalem.

Students could be given the following instructions:

- "Select one passage of Scripture to study further."

- "Consider the following questions as you read a passage from Acts describing a meeting in Jerusalem:

    Who were the persons involved?

    What was the reason for the meeting?

    What problems or conflicts were encountered?

    What decisions were made at the meeting?

    What happened after the meeting was over?

    What would you have done if you had attended that meeting?

- "After reading and reflecting, spend some time discussing your answers with others who selected the same passage."

- "Prepare a way to present 'your meeting' in a role play situation so that others will understand the issues that were dealt with in that meeting."

ACTIVITY NINE: WHAT DO WE DO NOW?

OBJECTIVE

At the end of the session the students should be able to suggest some of the alternative strategies the early Church adopted as it began to organize itself, and to select one strategy to identify with in a simulated way.

PROCESS

In the early years of the Church's history there were many different strategies that were considered and used in order to expand and extend the influence of Jesus' life and teachings. Some of these same strategies compete for the time, energy, money and commitment of Church people today. This activity will provide a way for students to identify some of the strategies that were considered by the early Church and use their own criteria to rank those strategies in order of priority for then and now.

The teacher will prepare a printed worksheet. (Printed on the following page.)

His Spirit fills us with power.   2 Timothy 1:7

What Do We Do Now?

We are followers of Jesus. Jesus has died but there have been experiences and reports of his renewed presence with some of his friends. We have waited in Jerusalem for seven weeks. Just yesterday, on the day of Pentecost, we were all together when we experienced a renewed power and life in a way we had never experienced before. God's Holy Spirit has blessed us with new excitement, energy, and hope. Today we are all together again. We are all asking ourselves and each other, "What do we do now?"

WHAT DO WE DO NOW? There are at least six possibilities. Rank the following in the order of their priority for you. (Rank your first choice No. 1 and the last choice No. 6.)

— I will write down some of the teachings of Jesus and important events of his life that I remember.

— I will speak to everyone and baptize those who believe that Jesus is the Messiah. I will go to the temple, the market place, everywhere.

— I will gather the disciples together. We need to organize ourselves, and to coordinate our efforts in fulfilling Jesus' Instructions.

— I will start right away healing the sick, clothing the needy, feeding the hungry, and visiting the lonely.

— I will work with others of the disciples to decide on standards for our new community to determine what others must believe and do in order to belong with us.

— I am not ready to do anything. I will go home to think it over.

Students can be given the following instructions:

- "Using the worksheet that is provided, by yourself, rank the six strategies in the order that you think would have been right for the early Church. Use whatever criteria you think is appropriate."

- When students have ranked the six items individually, then organize them into groups of three to five to compare their rankings and to decide on a concensus ranking for the group. If the group chooses the last one, "do nothing," then say to them, "Now that you have thought it over what will you do next?" That choice then becomes their highest.

- Each group shares with the whole class the concensus of their group.

- "Using your highest strategy (one of the first five, not the 'do nothing' choice) spend some time looking in Acts and also the writings of Paul to find examples of ways the the early Church acted out that strategy."

- Some follow-up activities:

    A. Obtain copies of the church budget, annual report, and monthly newsletters to see to what extent each of the five strategies is reflected in those written forms. This could provide an interesting way to evaluate the Church's ministry today.

    B. Encourage each group to participate in a project that would demonstrate the values of their highest ranking. For instance:

    ** "Write down the teaching" — students could write their own Gospel which could contain all that *they* remember about Jesus.

    ** "Speak to everyone" — students could decide what they want to tell others, then choose a place or group of people to go tell them about Jesus.

    ** "Get organized" — students could discuss together and draw up a plan of how their church ought to be organized today.

    ** "Help those in need" — students could identify some places in their own community where there are persons in need and plan a way to respond to at least one situation of need.

    ** "Decide on standards" — students could work up a list of standards of behavior and belief that should be required of everyone who wants to belong to the Church and be identified as Christian.

Focus On An Epistle

THE EPISTLE OF PAUL TO THE EPHESIANS

Introduction plus six activities . . .

** Some Questions to Consider

** Clues About the Apostle Paul

** Read With a Marking Pen

** Look for Something Specific

** Summarize With Several Key Words

** Connect the Epistle to a Song

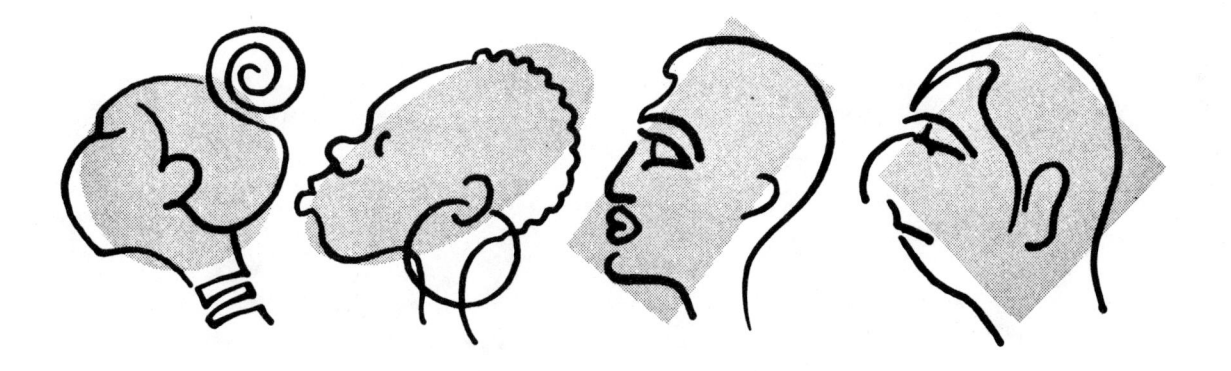

There is one body and one Spirit, just as there is one hope to which God has called you. There is one Lord, one faith, one baptism; there is one God and Father of all men, who is Lord of all, works through all, and is in all.

Ephesians 4:32

—41—

Eight: Focus On An Epistle

Usually in church education we introduce the Letters of the New Testament in a general way to older children but wait until the students are in youth or adult classes before we focus on the Letters in an intensive way. I personally think that this is a good strategy. So much of the language in Paul's letters is very abstract and difficult to comprehend unless a person has sufficient background and vocabulary and is able to deal with abstractions. Even for many older youth and adults the Letters are very difficult to comprehend.

What follows is a series of suggestions of ways to approach the study of one Epistle—The Letter of Paul to the Ephesians. Even though these suggestions focus on the specific Letter to the Ephesians some of the same approaches can be used or adapted in studying others of the New Testament Letters.

In study of any Letter it is very helpful to have one or more commentaries of the Bible to use. A commentary provides very helpful insights of scholars who have studied carefully the many aspects of biblical theology and interpretations. Some commentaries which may be helpful are listed in the Bibliography.

SOME QUESTIONS TO CONSIDER

As we have indicated in other activities it is often a good way to begin the study of a new subject by raising some very basic questions, then spending some time pursuing them. The teacher could raise his own questions to guide his study in preparation for teaching the subject. Or, the students as a group could state their questions to help them begin their study. Some questions which may be included are:

Who is the author of the Letter to the Ephesians?

> Even though Paul is traditionally identified as the author of the Ephesians, some New Testament scholars have questioned that claim.

To whom was the Letter written?

> The addressee is identified as the Ephesians, but who specifically was intended by the author?

What is the purpose of the Letter?

> Persons usually have reasons for writing their letters; why was this one written?

If the Letter was written by Paul, what previous contacts did he have with persons in Ephesus?

> By reading in the Letter itself or in the Book of Acts we can discover Paul's previous contacts with Eupesus.

What is the central theme or message of the Letter?

What theological questions are raised by reading the Letters?

What is similar and different between this Letter to the Ephesians and others of Paul's letters?

> (Others will think of additional questions that are important.)

CLUES ABOUT THE APOSTLE PAUL

Instead of reading Ephesians to discover what Paul's theological insights were, read the Letter in one sitting to see what you can discover about Paul as a person. There are many self-revealing statements that provide some insight about Paul as a person. A few of the statements are identified below, but there are others for you to discover for yourself.

    1:1   "From Paul, who by God's will is an apostle of Christ Jesus."

    1:16   "I remember you in my prayers."

    3:1   "I, Paul, the prisoner of Christ Jesus . . ."

    3:8   "I am less than the least of all God's people . . ."

If one were to read all the Letters of Paul looking for insight about Paul as a person one would be able to piece together a significant autobiography by Paul himself.

READ WITH A MARKING PEN

As you read through the whole Letter to the Ephesians read with a marking pen in hand to write marginal notes or questions or to underline significant statements that speak to you at the moment.

Read in a meditative spirit. Look for insight that you can apply directly to yourself in your present life situation. Underline these verses so that you can return to them. There may be just a few or many verses that you would underline. It all depends upon your present mood, needs, or questions. After you have finished reading the Letter, go back over the verses you underlined to contemplate them more thoroughly. Ask yourself the question, "If I were to apply what Paul says to my own life right now, what difference would it make in the way I live, in the decisions I make, and in the relationships I experience?" Spend a few moments in prayer seeking God's power to guide you in searching for the truth and applying it to your life.

You may also want to read with marking pen in hand to write question marks in the margin next to those verses that confuse you or with which you do not agree. These question marks could provide the focus for further exploration in a Bible commentary or for discussion with others.

LOOK FOR SOMETHING SPECIFIC

As you read the Letter to the Ephesians the first time you may get some impression of concepts that are being emphasized or specific concerns that are being developed. Read through the Letter a second time looking specifically for some of these key points. After I read through Ephesians once I wrote down a few things I wanted to look for more carefully in a second reading. Some of the things I looked for and what I found are:

Paul's description of the *Church* . . . .

    1:1   "God's people"

    1:23   "Christ's body"

    2:12   "God's chosen people"

    2:19   "family of God"

    2:21   "sacred temple"

. . . be kind and tender-hearted to one another, and forgive one another, as God has forgiven you in Christ.

Ephesians 4:32

Paul's instructions for living the *Christian life*. . . . .

    4:2   "Be humble, gentle, and patient. Show your love by being helpful to one another."
    4:3   "Do your best to preserve the unity which the Spirit gives."
    4:22   "Get rid of your old self . . . your hearts and minds must be made completely new."
    4:25   "No more lying."
    4:26   "If you become angry do not let your anger lead you into sin."
    4:26   "Do not stay angry all day."
    4:29   "Do not use harmful words in talking. Use only helpful words."
    5:2   "Your life must be controlled by love."

(And, there are many more passages that you can find.)

Paul's statements of the *actions of God and Jesus Christ* . . . .

    1:4   "Before the world was made, God had already chosen us to be his in Christ . . ."
    1:7   "For by the death of Christ we are set free and our sins are forgiven."
    2:8   "For it is by God's grace that you have been saved through faith. It is not your own doing, but God's gift."
    2:18   "It is through Christ that all of us, Jews and Gentiles, are able to come in the one Spirit into the presence of the Father."
    4:11   "It was he who gave gifts to men . . . he did this to prepare all God's people for the work of Christian service, to build up the body of Christ."

(And, you could find many more in your reading.)

Don't worry . . . but in all your prayers ask God for what you need.

PHILIPPIANS 4:6

SUMMARIZE WITH SEVERAL KEY WORDS

Each person who reads Paul's Letter to the Ephesians will be impressed and influenced in different ways. It is always a helpful process to try to summarize what one reads or hears by focusing his thoughts with a few key words. There are many key words that could be chosen, but I think it is most helpful to be selective and choose only a few that are most significant at the present time.

The key words that I chose after reading and studying the Letter to the Ephesians for a couple of days are:

"Oneness in Christ"

"New Life"

"God's work in Christ"

"Let us give thanks to God"

In order to complete the process the next step would be to use the above phrases as the beginning of a statement to which I would add my own words to make a complete statement. It is important that a person use his own words to complete the statement because that is how learning happens. Persons learn not because they remember something they read or hear. Rather, persons learn as a result of appropriating to themselves what is important and worth keeping. To reinforce that process it is more helpful to state in one's own words what he believes rather than reciting what someone else has said.

Put on all the armor that God gives you, so that you will stand up against the Devil's evil tricks.

Ephesians 6:11

CONNECT THE EPISTLE TO A SONG

As I was reading and rereading Paul's Epistle to the Ephesians the words to the song, "They'll Know We Are Christians By Our Love," kept coming to my mind. I was impressed by how many lines of that song connected directly with verses in the Epistle to the Ephesians. Because of my own interest in following through on this insight I discovered the following connections:

1. "We are one in the spirit, we are one in the Lord."

    4:4-6 "There is one body and one Spirit . . . there is one Lord, one faith, one baptism; there is one God and Father of all men."

    "We pray that all unity may one day be restored."

    4:3 "Do your best to preserve the unity which the Spirit gives, by the peace that binds you together."

2. "We will walk with each other, we will walk hand in hand."

    4:29   "Do not use harmful words in talking. Use only helpful words, the kind that build up and provide what is needed, so that what you say will do good to those who hear you."

"Together we will spread the news that God is in our Land."

    6:14   "So stand ready: have truth for a belt tight around your waist; put on righteousness for your breastplate, and the readiness to announce the Good News of peace as shoes for your feet."

3. "We will work with each other, we will work side by side."

    4:12   "He did this to prepare all God's people for the work of Christian service, to build up the body of Christ . . . ."

    4:16   "So when each separate part works as it should, the whole body grows and builds itself up through love."

"We'll guard each man's dignity and save each man's pride."

    4:24   "You must put on the new self, which is created in God's likeness, and reveals itself in the true life that is upright and holy."

4. "All praise to the Father from whom all things come."

    1:6   "Let us praise God for his glorious grace, for the free gift he gave us in dear Son."

"All praise to Christ Jesus, his only Son."

    2:18   "It is through Christ that all of us are able to come in the one Spirit into the presence of the Father."

"All praise to the Spirit who makes us one."

    2:22   "In union with him (Christ) you too are being built together with all the others into a house where God lives through his Spirit."

(Chorus) "And, they'll know we are Christians, by our love, by our love. Yes, they'll know we are Christians by our love."

    4:2   "Show your love by being helpful to one another."

    4:32   "Be kind and tender-hearted to one another and forgive one another, as God has forgiven you in Christ."

    5:2   "Your life must be controlled by Love."

A teacher could provide time for students to do for themselves what I did above. I was selective of passages to express what words of the song meant to me. Given the same song and the same Letter to the Ephesians other students would perhaps make different selections of verses. That is good. That demonstrates the richness of meaning in the words of the song and especially the words of Ephesians.

Something very important happens when a person participates in an activity such as this. Not only are the words of the song reinforced but there is great value in the process of searching through the Letter to the Ephesians to find appropriate verses. In this process persons are reading, reflecting, analyzing, comparing, interpreting and selecting verses of Scripture which goes a long way to reinforce new insights and learnings. Try it yourself!

After he had washed their feet, Jesus put his outer garment back on and returned to his place at the table. "Do you understand what I have just done to you?" he asked. "You call me Teacher and Lord, and it is right that you do so, because I am. I am your Lord and Teacher, and I have just washed your feet. You, then, should wash each other's feet. I have set an example for you, so that you will do just what I have done for you."

John 13:12-15

Using T.E.V. With Values Clarification Strategies

AN INTRODUCTION AND FIVE TEACHING ACTIVITIES

- ** The Values Sheet

- ** Values Voting

- ** Alternative Action Search

- ** Writing An Obituary

- ** What Will I do?

Nine: Using T.E.V. With Values Clarification Strategies

Introduction

Educators, pastors, parents and others in the Church have been concerned for centuries with teaching Christian values. Much preaching and teaching in the Church has focused upon the importance of adopting and living by values that are consistent with the life-style and teaching of the prophets in the Old Testament and with the life-style and teaching of Jesus Christ and the apostles in the New Testament.

In the Parable of the Two House Builders, Jesus said, "Those who hear my words and *do* them are like the wise man who built his house upon the rock." Again in Matthew's Gospel Jesus said, "As you *did* it to one of the least of these my brethren, you *did* it to me." At the conclusion of the Parable of the Good Samaritan Jesus says, "You go and *do* the same." The emphasis in each of these passages is upon *doing* what needs to be done to serve others, to put into action what one says he believes or thinks.

The Church in its education program has always been concerned to motivate persons to put into action their beliefs to behave in a way consistent with the teachings of Jesus Christ. The problem is that in the Church we have too often *told* persons what they *should* do. We have tended to moralize by imposing what we think is good or right or of value upon those we would teach. When one person implies that he knows what is right for another person and insists that the other person act accordingly, he is moralizing and taking the responsibility for deciding and acting away from him. The moralizing process does not help a person to become responsible, mature, and independent in his choosing and behaving.

Dr. Sidney Simon and his colleagues have suggested an alternative to moralizing in forming values. The process they propose is identified as *values clarification*. This approach to forming values places a lot of trust upon the other person. The process says that there are many divirgent, competitive, alternate values and that persons must choose for themselves how they are going to live their lives and be responsible for those choices. It does not mean that adult teachers or parents ignore the students, or leave them completely on their own to decide. Rather, adults provide a climate, a structure and ways of interacting with students that help them to experience the seven steps of value formation.

In recent years there has developed a particular approach to teaching values in public schools which has been closely identified with Sidney Simon and what he calls "values clarification." It is interesting to me that from the public education sector we in the Church are finding direction and support for our task of teaching values. In what follows I have depended quite heavily upon the experience and writings of Sidney Simon, especially his two books *Values and Teaching* and *Values Clarification*. I have attempted to adapt what was originally designed for public school teachers and to apply the concepts and strategies to church education.

A. *Seven Steps of Value Formation*

   DEFINITION

   Values are those elements that *show* how a person has *decided* to use his life.

   PROCESS OF VALUING

   According to Sidney Simon, unless something satisfies *all* seven of the criteria we do not call it a value.

1. *Choosing Freely* — Values must be freely selected if they are to be really valued by the individual.
2. *Choosing From Among Alternatives* — Only when choice is possible, with more than one alternative from which to choose, do we say a value can result.
3. *Choosing After Thoughtful Consideration of the Consequences of Each Alternative* — A value can emerge only with thoughtful consideration of the range of alternatives and consequences in a choice.
4. *Prizing and Cherishing* — Values flow from choices we are glad to make.
5. *Affirming* — We are willing to affirm publicly our values.
6. *Acting Upon Choices* — For a value to be present, life itself must be affected. Nothing can be a value that does not, in fact, give direction to actual living.
7. *Repeating* — Values tend to have a persistency, tend to make a pattern in a life.

B. *Values and Value Indicators*

According to the seven steps identified above, many things that we have thought to be values are not really values but rather *value indicators*. Our values usually grow out of what are identified as value indicators. The following ten categories are important aspects of a person's life but ordinarily do not fulfill all seven steps, or criteria, of value formation.

1. Goals or purposes
2. Aspirations
3. Attitudes
4. Interests
5. Feelings
6. Beliefs, convictions, ideas
7. Opinions, points of view
8. Activities
9. Worries, problems, obstacles
10. Likes or dislikes, preferences

A value indicator such as a belief may satisfy the first five criteria, but unless someone acts upon his belief it is not a value; it is only a value indicator. A person's belief indicates what has the potential to become a value but it is not a value until it shows how he has decided to use his life.

C. *Value-Rich Areas of Life*

All persons have some values. They may not be able to articulate what their values are, but if they are making choices between alternative actions they do have values. The values clarification approach is a way to help persons identify, clarify, formulate, and express their own personal values.

There are some areas in our lives that are especially significant, that require of us to formulate some values.

1. *Money* — how it is obtained, used, treated.
2. *Friendship* — how we relate to other persons.
3. *Love and sex* — how we deal with intimate, sexual relationships.
4. *Religion* — what we hold as our basic beliefs.
5. *Leisure* — how we spend our free time.
6. *Politics and social organization* — who we vote for, how agencies are organized, what laws they pass.
7. *Work* — choice of vocation, time, energy spent working, attitudes towards work.
8. *Family* — how one behaves in relationships with parents, siblings, children, etc.
9. *Maturity* — what each person strives for to be responsible, independent, grown-up.
10. *Character traits* — what persons are like, the ways they behave.

D. Jesus' Values and My Values From the New Testament

If a person desires to learn more about what Sidney Simon and his colleagues present in the way of rationale, strategies, and descriptions of research projects, I would recommend two very valuable books, *Values and Teaching* and *Values Clarification*. (See Bibliography for more information.)

In the book *Values Clarification* there are presented seventy-nine different, useable strategies that can be used in the classroom to help students work through the process of values clarification. Values clarification is not intended to be curriculum in itself, but rather a supplement to the prescribed, on-going curriculum.

Even though the seventy-nine strategies were designed for use by public school teachers I was impressed with the possibility of translating some of the strategies into the church education scene and adapting them to teach Scripture.

There are a variety of ways to approach the study of Jesus' life and teachings that will help students focus on Jesus' values as well as their own values. Too often we are satisfied to teach events, dates, places, persons and all the facts related to each. To collect or remember a lot of information is only a preliminary step to learning. There are other more significant steps that contribute much more to the learning process. Comparing, illustrating, restating in their own words, using personal examples, applying to personal life situations are the steps beyond collecting and remembering. Many of the values clarification strategies could be adapted and applied to Jesus' life and teachings in order to help the students identify with Jesus more personally.

1. *The Value Sheet* — A Value Sheet is something that teachers can prepare for students to work on individually or in small groups. A Value Sheet is a list of thought-provoking questions based upon a statement, story, question, issue, or event that causes persons to make choices that reflect on their values. What follows is a sample Value Sheet and a list of criteria to consider in designing Value Sheets.

   Use some of Jesus' actions or teachings to set the stage for developing a series of questions that form a values sheet.

Read the Parable of the Good Samaritan in Luke 10:25-37. *Think about,* then *write* or *discuss* responses to the following questions —

   (a) What do you think about the action of the Priest and the Levite?

   (b) The Samaritan was considered an enemy to the Hebrews. Why do you think he stopped?

   (c) If you were the injured person, how would you feel about the Samaritan?

   (d) What are some examples from your own experience that are similar to this story Jesus told?

   (e) Jesus told the parable in response to the question, "Who is my neighbor?" How would you answer that question?

   (f) Think of someone you know who needs a neighbor. How can you be a neighbor to that person?

Several criteria to consider when constructing Value Sheets:

- Do the questions allow for free choice?
- Does the teacher's judgment shine through the questions? If so, reword the questions so that they do not moralize or imply obvious right answers.
- Are the questions focused upon areas about which the students have some very definite feelings?
- Does the list of questions relate to some of the seven steps in the valuing process?
- Is there at least one question that encourages the student to reflect on his own action?
- Is the climate such that students feel free to make personal choices and will be accepted no matter what the choice?

2. *Values Voting* — Without announcing the source of the topics to vote on, select some examples of Jesus' sayings and actions. Present them to the class for voting, prefacing each with "How many of you . . .?" Record the votes. After voting turn to the Scriptures to find the references to see how Jesus "voted" in terms of his action. Discuss why they think Jesus "voted" the way he did. What were his values?

Sample questions based upon the Sermon on the Mount:

- How many of you believe that God will reward those persecuted and insulted because of their commitment to Jesus? (Matt. 5:11-12)
- How many of you think that the person who hates another person is just as guilty as the one who kills another? (Matt. 5:21-22)
- How many of you agree that a man who looks at a woman and wants to possess her is guilty of committing adultery? (Matt. 5:27-28)
- How many of you feel that it is right to not take revenge on someone who wrongs us? (Matt. 5:38-42)
- How many of you think that love for a friend is better than love for an enemy? (Mat. 5:43-47)
- How many of you think that a person can love God and money too? (Matt. 6:24)

3. *Alternative Action Search* — Read one or another of the following incidents in Jesus' life:

- Jesus' temptation in the wilderness.
- Jesus' encounter with the Pharisees.
- Jesus' trial before the High Priest or Pilate.

Conclude the reading just prior to where it states what Jesus' response or action was. Then have students list all the possible alternatives, select the actions they would consider taking, then compare their choices with the choice Jesus made.

Other Examples:

Read Matthew 11:1-4a

** List all the possible answers Jesus could make.
** What would you say if you were Jesus?
** Compare with Jesus' answer, Matthew 11:4-6.

Read Mark 14:53-61

** List all of the alternative actions Jesus could take.

** Select the one you would take.

** Compare your selection with what Jesus did do.

4. *Writing an Obituary* — After a study of Jesus' life and teaching, encourage students to write an obituary for Jesus by completing any or all of the following (or creating more of their own).

> Jesus, 33, died yesterday from . . .
>
> He is survived by . . .
>
> He was a member of . . .
>
> At the time of his death he was working on . . .
>
> He will be remembered for . . .
>
> He will be mourned by . . . because . . .
>
> The world will suffer from his loss because . . .
>
> He always wanted, but never got to . . .
>
> The body will be . . .
>
> In lieu of flowers . . .

After each student has written his own obituary for Jesus, it will be very interesting to compare them. What students will be doing is identifying what they consider to be of value in Jesus' life.

5. *What will I do?* There are many instances in the Gospels where Jesus encounters individuals or groups of persons. In most of these the response of the people is stated. The teacher could read or have printed on a transparency or stencil the situation of Jesus' encounter with the persons without presenting the person's response. The students could take the role of the person, then list the possible alternative actions and proceed with the Alternative Action Search format.

Examples:

Read Mark 10:17-21

** List the possible responses this man could make.

Read Mark 14:66-67

** List possible responses of Peter.

Read Matthew 16:13

** List possible answers to Jesus' question.

Use the Overhead Projector With T.E.V.

** Instead of A Chalkboard

** Student Reports

** Student Creativity

** Map Study

** Enlarging Printed Materials

** Projecting Words of Songs

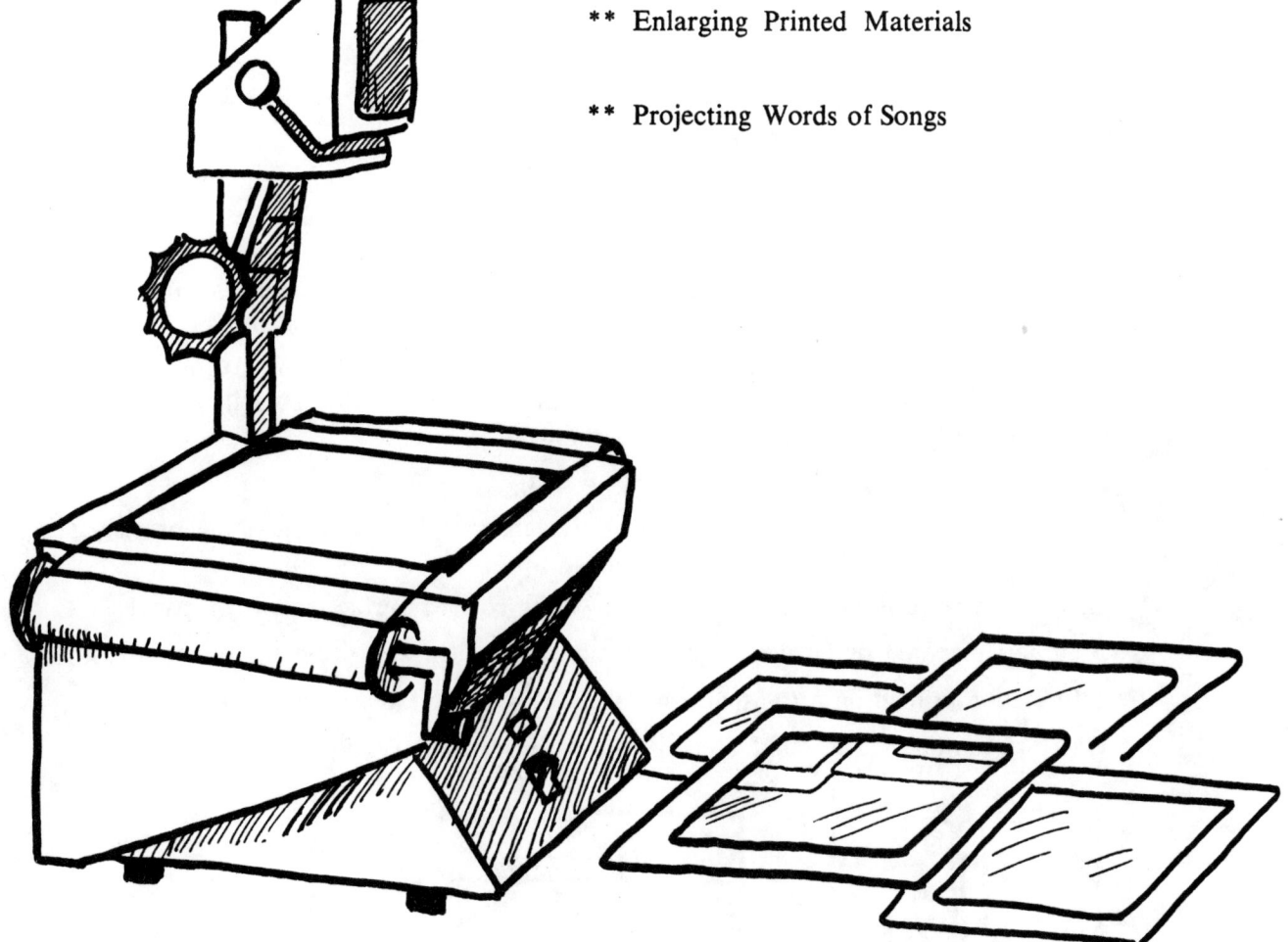

Ten: Use The Overhead Projector With T.E.V.

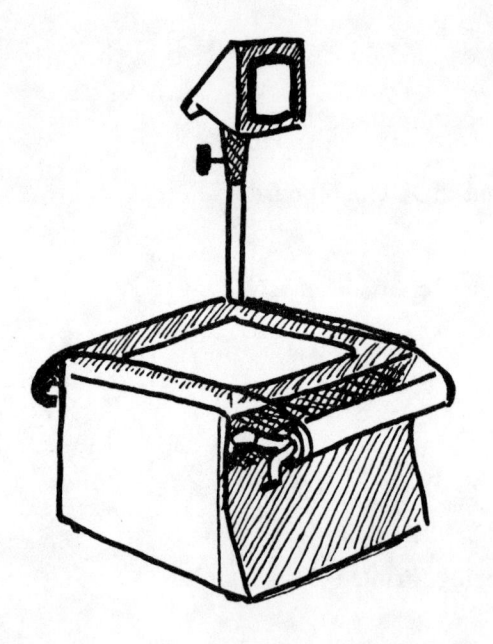

The overhead projector is becoming one of the most useful pieces of audio-visual equipment available to teachers in churches. In 1968 when I first conducted teacher training workshops throughout Northern California, I knew of only two or three churches that owned overhead projectors. Today I am aware of more than one hundred churches that own a projector and there are many more churches that would have one if they could afford it.

Before presenting six different ways to use the overhead projector with T.E.V. in the church classroom we should consider briefly some advantages and disadvantages to the overhead projector.

There are many advantages to the overhead projector which include:

** Room need not be darkened. All overhead projectors project with a bright enough image to be used in a lighted room.

** The projector is used in front of the room by teacher and students. When using the projector the teacher faces the class, maintaining continual eye contact with the students.

** The operation of an overhead projector is so simple that anyone can use it. All it takes is a little practice to become familiar with the simple steps: plug it in, turn it on, focus it with easily accessible knob, and use it.

** A large 10 x 10 inch writing surface is provided.

** Materials can be prepared ahead of time by teachers and students at home or elsewhere.

** Images can be projected on a screen or any light-colored surface, wall, or panel.

** Materials prepared by teachers and students can be filed and saved for future use.

** Information printed on a transparency can be exposed to the class one line at a time.

** Overlays can be used to build up or break down a complex subject.

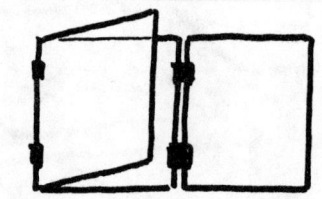

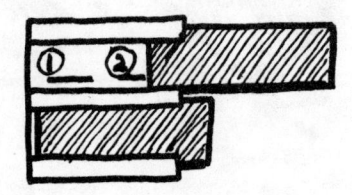

** There is a tremendous visual impact because of the large bright image and the color and variety of materials that are projected.

In my experience there are only three disadvantages that I can think of that might concern someone who is considering purchase or use of an overhead projector.

- ** The cost of purchasing an overhead projector stands in the way of many churches with limted budgets. I personally would not spend more than $200.00 for a good overhead projector plus roll attachment with acetate roll, dust cover, starter pack of transparencies, and pack of projection pens. Usually one can find an excellent projector and supplies for less than $200.00.

- ** Materials must be transparent. This means that everything used on the overhead projector must be prepared in some transparent form. Some materials and teaching activities are not easily presented in that format.

- ** Teachers and students must spend time preparing all of their own materials. There are very, very few commercially-prepared transparencies for church education and those that are available are very expensive. In my experience of using an overhead projector for many years I have found that students respond much more favorably to teacher and student prepared materials than they do to those produced commercially.

There are many, many creative ways to use an overhead projector in the classroom. What follows is a summary of six of the more common ways to use it with some specific suggestions for teaching the New Testament in church education.

INSTEAD OF A CHALKBOARD

Personally, I would invest in an overhead projector if I used it in no other way than as a substitute for a chalkboard. When using a chalkboard the teacher must turn his back to the students when writing. Whenever the teacher turns his back he is losing contact with the class. With the overhead projector the teacher faces the class and can maintain visual contact.

Once the teacher has covered all the space on the chalkboard he must erase part of what is written in order to add something new. With an overhead projector it is just a matter of exchanging transparencies in just a few seconds.

Many times the teacher wastes his, and the students', time while he writes material on the chalkboard. With projection pens and sheets of acetate a teacher or student could prepare material ahead of time to avoid any waste of time during the class.

As a substitute for a chalkboard an overhead projector can be used in the following ways:

- ** Teacher can prepare instructions for class activities and project them for all to see instead of depending upon students to receive and remember the instructions from an oral presentation.

    Using an activity from *Focus on the Acts of the Apostles* section of this book instructions could be printed on a transparency. By having all the instructions written out and visual to all students they will be able to work at their own pace. The teacher will not have to continually repeat the instructions as students finish each step. This frees the teacher to relate more directly with individual students and provides students with a sense of independence and security in the awareness that they know what they are supposed to be doing.

The following instructions could be printed on a transparency:

Do the following . . . .

Step One: Select the name of one apostle on which to do some further research.

Step two: Use the books on the resource table to search for information about your person.

Step three: As you are reading, consider these questions:

- What does the apostles name mean?

- How did he first encounter Jesus?

- What special things did the apostle do?

- What kind of relationship did he have with Jesus?

- What kind of person was the apostle?

- What influence did he have on the early Church?

Step four: Summarize what you have learned about your apostle by writing a letter as if it were a letter of introduction to someone else.

** In an activity where the teacher and students are developing a list of items in response to a question or instruction, it is much better to write the responses down for all to see rather than depending upon persons to remember what they hear.

For example: The teacher could give the instruction, "Let's make a list of all the possible actions the disciples could have taken immediately after Jesus' crucifixion." The students would have a lot of suggestions. Each suggestion should be written down exactly as stated by the students. After the list is completed and is visible for all to see, it could be used by the teacher to involve students in further discussion.

- When you see all of these possible actions, what impressions or insights do you have?

- Let's organize all the suggestions into three or four categories. What are some possible categories?

- Which of the actions did the disciples take?

- Which action would you have taken if you had been one of the disciples?

The discussion that follows the initial activity of listing all the possible actions is enhanced by having the responses visible for all to see.

** In Chapter Two we suggested the activity of reading the definition of "disciple" in the T.E.V. WORD LIST, then stating some questions that come to mind. The overhead projector could be used to record those questions for all to see.

** Teachers can prepare ahead of time an outline of the main points of a presentation they want to make to the class. By using a piece of 8½ x 11 inch white paper, laying it over the transparency, it is possible to expose one line or item at a time because the white paper blocks out the light and everything not covered by the white paper is projected on the screen. Also, the white paper is translucent enough for the teacher to see what is under it, without it being projected, so that the teacher can see what is coming next on the transparency.

STUDENT REPORTS

Students working individually or in small groups can prepare reports, summaries, or presentations to share with the rest of the class. These reports could be prepared during the class period or at home.

An experience in our family illustrates this activity very well. Several years ago when Scott was in the fifth grade he was given a social studies assignment of preparing a notebook on the State of Maine. We had been to Maine the previous summer so he was highly motivated to share what he knew and to find out more about Maine. However, when he was told the form in which the report had to be submitted he became less motivated. He really did not want to do another notebook like every fifth grader had done in that class. After some conversation with Scott, we came up with the idea of asking his teacher if he could prepare the report on transparencies so that he could present it on the overhead projector.

Fortunately the teacher was open enough to agree to this request. Scott spent hours preparing a dozen or more transparencies, several with overlays. Later in conversation with Scott's teacher she said to me, "I am glad that Scott wanted to make his social studies report on the overhead projector. We have one in class all the time but I never realized before that the students could use it too."

The next time the students were given a similar assignment, a half dozen of them wanted to use the overhead projector. Instead of being surprised that the students can and want to use an overhead projector, we should help them see this as a very useful resource that they can use whenever it is appropriate.

There are several ways that students can prepare reports, summaries, or presentations on the overhead projector.

** Instead of writing a summary on a piece of paper to read to the class, the student could print it on a transparency and project it for the whole class to read.

** If three small groups are each working to find information or answers to the same subject, each group could be given one transparency with one-third of the space blocked off in which they would write their information. Three transparencies would be used, each with a different third of it blocked off. When the groups are finished and ready to present their findings to the rest of the class the first group would place its transparency on the projector. After group one is done, then the second group would place its transparency on top of the first one, and the third group likewise. In the end all three groups' reports would be simultaneously visible to everyone else. This is a very efficient and effective way to share the results of several groups' work.

** Another variation of the above activity is to assign two or more groups different biblical passages that deal with the same event or teaching. For example: Matthew 28, Luke 16, Luke 24, and John 20 all focus on the disciples' experience of Jesus' resurrection. Two or more of the Gospels can be compared by having each group answer identical questions based on what they read in their chapter. Questions could include:

- Who went to the tomb?

- What did they discover there?

- Whom did they meet?

- What were they told about Jesus?

- What were their responses?

- What was their experience of the risen Lord?

Each group on the blocked off section of its transparency could record the answers to the questions. Then the four transparencies, with four sets of answers, can be projected simultaneously so that students can compare easily the similarities and differences between the four Gospels. Wherever there are cross references listed for a passage, this activity could be used. The primary requirement is an appropriate question or list of questions to guide the students in their searching.

STUDENT CREATIVITY

We have taken for granted that paper, pencils, crayons, and paints can be used by students to express themselves creatively. Blank transparencies plus projection pens and pencils can also be used by students and teachers to express themselves in creative ways as they seek to communicate a visual interpretation of a subject of Scripture. There are many, many ways for students to use the overhead projector in creative activities. The three or four ways that are described in what follows will suggest other possibilities to you.

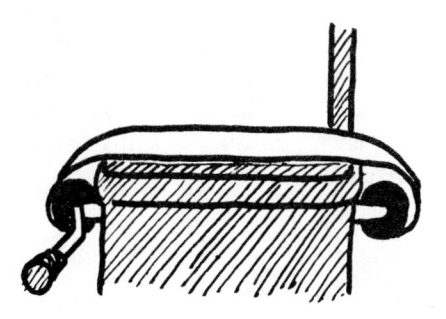

** With a roll of acetate attached to the overhead projector, students could create a series of visuals to present a story. The students could tell their story verbally as they roll the acetate to project their illustrations one after the other.

** Students could outline five squares on a blank transparency. In the middle square they could trace one of the line drawings from T.E.V. Then in the first two squares they could create their own line drawings to depict what preceded the one they traced. And, in the last two squares they could create what follows. The result would be a five-frame study, created and interpreted by the students in response to one of the events in the New Testament.

** Another way to use a line drawing is to trace it on to a transparency to use as the central focus for a larger drawing that the student would complete in his own way.

** Opaque puppets can be created by using stiff paper or cardboard from which to cut profiles or silhouettes of faces, persons, or objects. By attaching the jaw of a face with a paper fastener it is possible to simulate talking. The opaque silhouette puppets project as black images on the screen. This is a fun and unique way to create a puppet presentation.

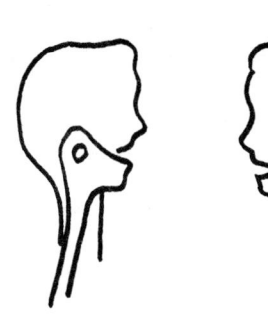

** The overhead projector makes a good light source for shadow play.

MAP STUDY

The overhead projector is an excellent resource to use with map studies. By tracing maps from atlases it is possible to project on the screen any map that is printed in a book. By the use of several transparencies in the overlay technique it is possible to build on a basic map additional information and concepts. The teacher could start with just a black line outline of the Mediterranean Sea and adjacent countries. On a second transparency the names of the countries and major cities could be printed. On a third transparency the cities Paul visited on one of his journeys could be circled in red. And on the fourth transparency, lines could be drawn to connect the cities in the order in which Paul visited them. Instead of students having to perceive all the information and concepts on one printed map it is possible in this process to develop one concept at a time.

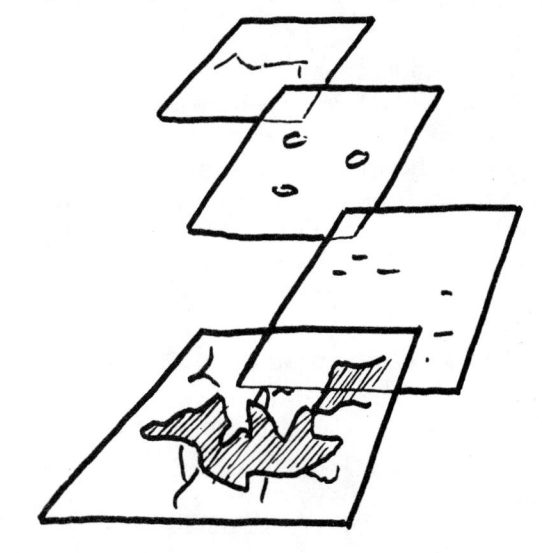

In *Chapter Seven: Focus On the Acts of the Apostles* there is a map of the Mediterranean countries. Following are two additional maps. These maps can be used to trace on transparencies. Names of countries, cities and bodies of water are purposely omitted so that teachers and students can use them in a variety of different ways. If the map is torn from the book it can be used with a sheet of thermal transparency in a thermal copier to produce a transparent map identical to the printed map. (See chapter 15 for additional instructions.)

ENLARGING PRINTED MATERIALS

An overhead projector is an easy way to enlarge drawings, maps, symbols, diagrams, or other printed materials for which an enlargement is desired. Use, for example, a line drawing from T.E.V.

** Trace the line drawing on a transparency with black projection pen or pencil.

** Project transparency on a sheet of newsprint, poster board, cloth, burlap, felt, or other material on which the drawing will be done.

** Trace the projected lines with felt pen.

The enlarged line drawings can be used as an outline for stitchery or yarn to make a banner, a poster, a teaching picture, or outline for a mosaic.

Enlarged maps would provide space for small groups of students to add new material, draw illustrations, or write information that is not possible on an 8½ x 11 inch map.

PROJECTING WORDS OF SONGS

Many times students are inhibited in their singing if they do not have hymnals with which to follow the words. And, most classrooms do not have hymnals for each of the students. We have had experiences of making large-print song charts on poster board or butcher paper so that students could follow the words. The same thing can be accomplished by printing the words of a song on a transparency and projecting them on a screen or on the wall. If the roll attachment is used, each verse of a song can be written separately, then the roll advanced as the song is sung.

Another activity that is similar is when we play a recording of a song to listen to the words and music. Most persons are helped if they can visualize the words at the same time as they hear them. The words of a song could be printed ahead of time and projected while the recording is being played.

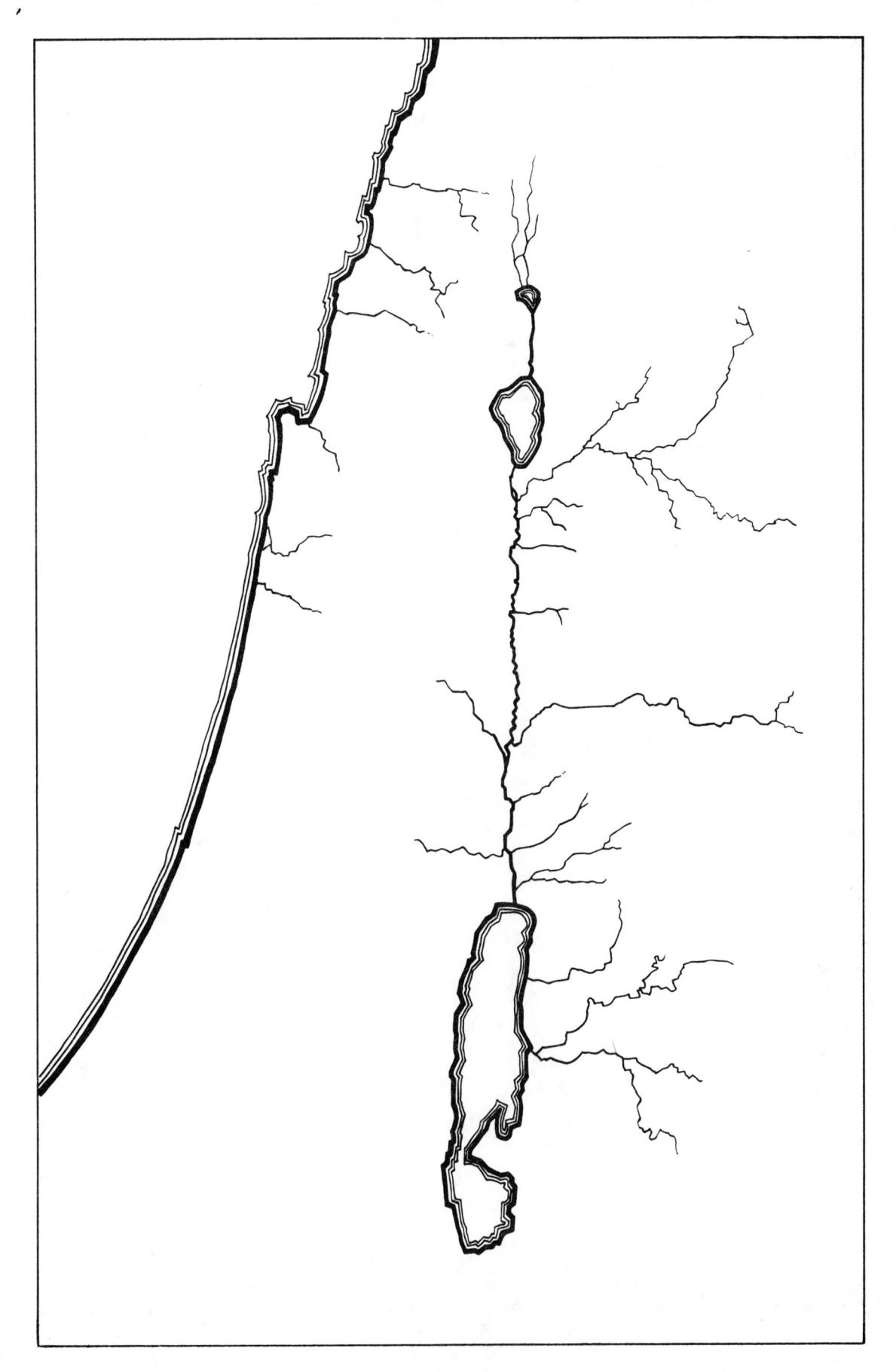

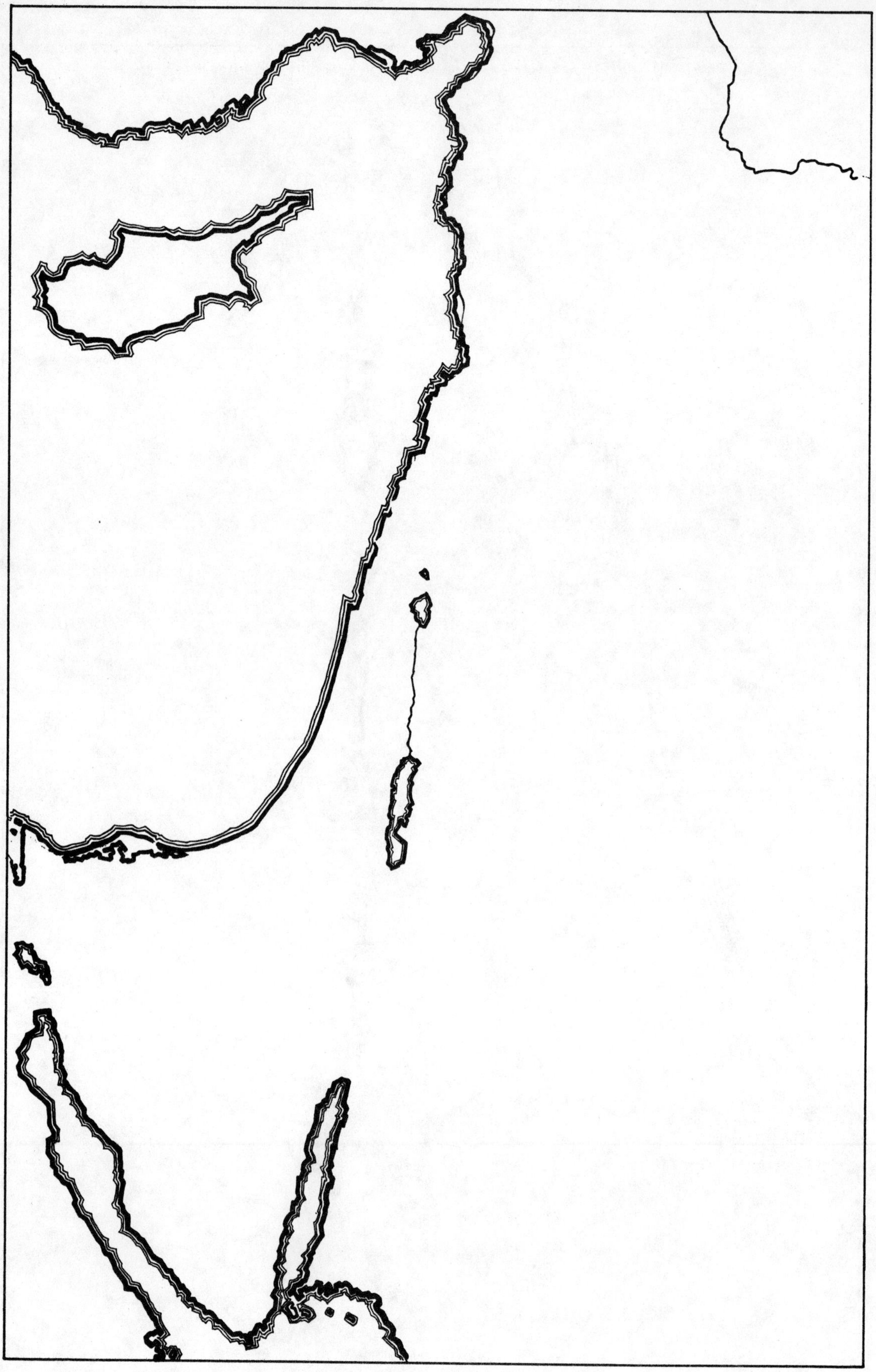

Use the Cassette Recorder With T.E.V.

** T.E.V. on Cassette Tapes

** Students Interview Others

** Reports and Answers from Pastors

** Instructions for Student Activities

** Students' Questions, Statements and Creativity

** Commercially Produced Tapes

Eleven: Use The Cassette Recorder With T.E.V.

Perhaps the most available, inexpensive piece of audio-visual equipment is the cassette tape recorder. Some children and youth receive cassette recorders for birthday and Christmas presents. Adults use cassette tapes as a means of correspondence instead of writing letters. A good quality, reliable cassette recorder can be purchased for $60.00. Such an inexpensive recorder will serve well most of the functions for which a teacher will use it. However, if quality sound is desired from recording or playing music, then a more expensive, better quality recorder will be required. Not only are there many commercially produced cassette tapes which can be used as resources in church education, but creative teachers and students are discovering dozens of exciting ways to use the cassette recorder in their teaching and learning activities.

Before exploring six ways of using the cassette recorder with T.E.V. we should first consider some of the advantages and disadvantages of cassette recorders and tapes.

Some of the *advantages* include:

** Tape recording with cassettes is a quick, simple operation. All cassette tapes are standard size and work in every cassette recorder. There is no way a cassette tape can be inserted wrong.

** The recorders are very portable. They usually have fitted cases with attached carrying straps. Most recorders can be operated with batteries which means they can be used outside or any other place without worrying about electrical power. Some (usually more expensive) recorders have built-in condenser microphones.

** Cassette tapes can be edited so that mistakes are easily corrected. They can be re-used without loss of quality and can be stored and filed easily.

** Cassette tapes can be used by individuals, small groups, and large groups.

** Cassette recorders and tapes are very flexible and can be used in a wide variety of creative ways.

There are several *disadvantages* to using cassette recorders:

** Cassette recordings are exclusively an audio device, which in a visually oriented world does not have the communicating effectiveness of other visual media. However, cassette recordings can be used with visual materials and become very valuable.

** Difficulties may occur in trying to locate the exact spot on the tape where material is to be selected for replay. This problem is eliminated when the recorder has a digital counter and the tape has been timed in advance.

** A lot of time is required to prepare for and record effective instructional tapes.

** Teachers and students may treat the tape recorder as a novelty or extra resource to be used during free time or for just fun activities.

When I weigh the disadvantages against the advantages, and realize that I can change all the disadvantages, then I am convinced that with a cassette recorder I have the potential of a very valuable resource.

On the next several pages I will suggest six specific ways that cassette recorders and tapes can be used in teaching activities that focus on the New Testament. These six suggestions are taken from a list of thirty different activities that require use of a cassette recorder.

T.E.V. ON CASSETTE TAPES

The American Bible Society has produced a series of fifteen cassette tapes that include the recording of the entire New Testament (see Bibliography). Nowhere can one buy C-60 cassette tapes for $2.50 that are already recorded. This has to be one of the best bargains of our day. I think every church should have at least one set of these tapes in their library. The reading voice on the tapes is easy to listen to and very expressive of the drama of the narrative. I have used excerpts from these tapes in a variety of ways and I am sure that you will think of other ways to use them.

** For personal use one could listen to the tapes while driving, working in the kitchen or garage, or relaxing.

** Persons who are homebound, in the hospital, or who have difficulty reading would find the recording of T.E.V. very inspiring to them in their situation of need.

** In the classroom the teacher could use the recordings of T.E.V. with individual or small groups of students who are not skillful readers.

** On several occasions I have used the recording of the text of a parable to serve as a narration for a filmstrip.

** If a church has a set of T.E.V. cassettes in the church library they could be checked out by families to use in their homes for regular family devotions or on special occasions.

** When teachers prepare self-instructional tapes for students to use individually or in small groups they could include a passage from the recorded T.E.V. This would add the variety of another voice to the tape instead of the teacher reading the text.

STUDENTS INTERVIEW OTHERS

When students are studying particular parts of the Scripture they are helped when they hear not only the teacher's interpretation and their own opinions, but when they can be exposed to the points of view of other persons. One way to gather a number of points of view of others is to use the interview technique. Students need some preparation to conduct interviews with other persons. They should follow some very basic steps:

1. Practice with the cassette recorder so that it can be operated flawlessly.

2. Team up with another person to work together in conducting the interviews.

3. Practice interviewing other students in the same class.

4. Decide on one or two carefully worded questions.

5. Decide on a time and place to interview persons.

6. Approach people in a way like this: "Good morning, I am John Smith. We are working on a project in our sixth grade church school class. We are studying about Jesus' life and teachings and we want to hear what other persons think. May I ask you a question to record your answer for our class?"

7. Conduct the interviews but do not record the question each time. Ask the question, then start the recording.

After the students have had some practice in the classroom and by working in teams of two they should feel able to interview persons. When they have done it several times, then they will become even more comfortable.

Not every New Testament subject is appropriate for this activity so some discretion should be used when deciding to guide the students in the interviewing process. Also, this process should not be overused. If one class were to do it once or twice a year, that might be enough.

The following are samples of the types of questions that could be asked of persons as they are coming to church on a Sunday morning by students from a class:

- When you hear the words "disciple" and "discipleship" what are some things that you think of?

- What is your favorite part of the Bible? Why?

- What is one question that comes to mind about what Jesus said or did?

- When you think of Jesus what is the first impression or image that comes to mind?

- What are three words you would use to describe Jesus?

- If you would select one teaching of Jesus to emphasize in your life what would it be?

Asking the same question of six to ten persons should be enough for using in the class later. It may be that after the students have had some experience with the process of asking questions that they would be able to conduct a two to five minute interview using a conversation technique.

When the students return to class they could listen to the recorded tape all the way through the first time. After some discussion and perhaps some questions of their own they could listen to all or part of the tape a second time to notice specific comments or insights. During the second playing of the recording it would be helpful to stop the tape at strategic places to allow time for further discussion.

REPORTS AND ANSWERS FROM PASTORS

In most churches it is very difficult for pastors to be directly involved in what happens in the classrooms of children and youth. The cassette recorder is one way to bring the pastor into the classroom. If the students are studying a subject that raises a lot of questions in their minds it would be possible to make a list of those questions and give it to the pastor and ask him to present his answers on a cassette recording that can be shared with the class the following week. Or, it would even be better if the teacher with several students were to make a half-hour appointment with the pastor during the week and then present their questions in person and have some time of discussion with the pastor which could all be recorded for later use in the class. It should be obvious that what is recorded once can be filed and stored for subsequent use by other classes or groups or by the same teacher at another time.

INSTRUCTIONS FOR STUDENT ACTIVITIES

When one teacher works with a class of fifteen or more students there are many times when it is desirable for the students to work at different tasks in small groups. It is not easy for one teacher to provide instructions and supervision for two or more groups simultaneously. However, with use of a cassette recorder it is almost as if the teacher had an assistant because it is possible to be in more than one place and do more than one thing at a time. The teacher could describe to the whole class generally what is offered in the two groups which he has planned. Then he could say to the students:

"Those of you who have chosen the activities of . . . will go to the table over there. Notice there is a tape recorder there. You have learned how to operate it before, so just turn it on and then follow the instructions that are recorded there."

When teachers provide students with opportunities to make choices and trust them to fulfill what is expected of them in those choices they will seldom be disappointed by the behavior or the achievement of the students.

There are many subjects and strategies that can be developed for self-instructional activities and implemented with a cassette tape recorder. There are several hints that might be helpful to teachers as they prepare for such activities:

1. Focus on a specific subject area or skill in which the students will be involved.

2. Start the tape with a brief introduction of what students can expect.

3. It is helpful to have other materials at hand to use while listening: a map, paper and pencil, a worksheet, a Bible, other books, a picture, etc.

4. In addition to having instructions recorded it is helpful for most students if they can also see the instructions written down someplace.

5. After giving instructions on the tape for the students to do something, then be very directive by recording the following: "Turn the tape recorder off while you work. If you have any questions, ask me. When you are finished with your work, turn the recorder on again."

6. If questions are asked or instructions are given for a simple activity like turning to a specific page, finding a Bible passage, or writing down a few words, be sure to pause on the tape in order to allow sufficient time for the students to do what is expected.

With a little bit of practice and willingness to experiment, teachers will find that the involvement and motivation of the students increases and also their own effectiveness increases through this technique of self-instructional activities guided by cassette recording.

STUDENTS' QUESTIONS, STATEMENTS AND CREATIVITY

There are many ways the cassette recorder can be used by the students to record their own materials.

** In addition to recording questions to present to someone else to answer, they could record their questions at the beginning of a unit of study, then listen to their own questions in a summary session at the end of the unit to see how many questions remain unanswered.

** Some students are more able to express themselves verbally than they are able to write a composition. For those students it would be desirable to have a cassette recorder available so that they can express their insights in that format.

** Students could write, then record, narrations for puppet plays and other dramatic activities. Sometimes it is easier to plan ahead what to say, record it, then use it for the drama instead of trying to think of what to say on the spot.

** Many filmstrips are visually suggestive of the subject intended so that even without a script it is possible to interpret the filmstrip. With such filmstrips the students can prepare their own script and record it to present to the whole class with the filmstrips.

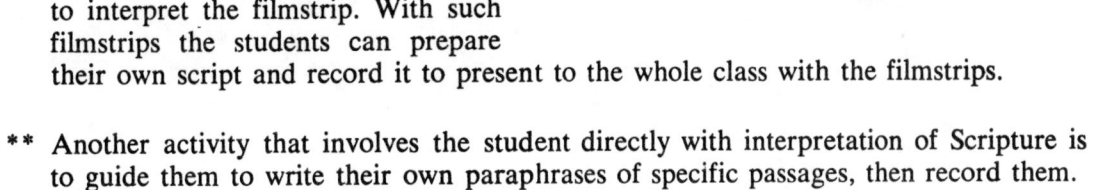

** Another activity that involves the student directly with interpretation of Scripture is to guide them to write their own paraphrases of specific passages, then record them.

COMMERCIALLY PRODUCED TAPES

In addition to the cassette tapes produced by the American Bible Society there are some other sources of prerecorded tapes that can be used effectively in the classroom. (See Bibliography for addresses of sources.)

** Many producers of filmstrips now package filmstrips with long-play record or cassette tape. Where there is a choice, I would always prefer a tape to a phonograph record. They are easier to file and store. And, they are easier to use in the classroom.

** *Cokesbury Bookstores* feature a series of cassette tapes by Dennis Benson that can be used with youth and adult classes or groups. A series identified as SOS (Switched On Scripture) includes several tapes related to the New Testament: *Acts: Part I or DDT* (Daring, Delightful, Threatening); *Acts: Part II or COD* (Christians on Demand); *Yin-Yang or 1st John;* and *Faith That Works or James*. Each of these cassettes is a collection of recorded resources that can be used directly in leading a class or group for three to six sessions.

** *Avant Garde Records* has reproduced a number of outstanding phonograph records in the cassette format. Among those available are several by the Medical Mission Sisters: *Joy Is Like the Rain, Knock, Knock!,* and *I Know the Secret,* and others such as *Follow Me, Go Tell Everyone, Busy Day* and more.

** *Thesis Tapes* has produced a series titled *Faith Alive*. There are ten separate tapes now available, six of them on New Testament subjects. Each tape includes four Bible dramas done in a style that gives the feeling of "You Are There." Any of these tapes is appropriate for elementary to adult students. One part of a tape could be incorporated into a larger, more complete lesson plan.

** Music such as *Jesus Christ, Superstar; Godspell;* and other contemporary and classical music are available from local record stores on cassette tapes.

Use the Slide Projector With T.E.V.

** Introduction

** Do-It-Yourself Write-On Slides

** Slides From Bible Lands

** Illustrate Scripture With Slides

** Photograph Line Drawings

Twelve: Use The Slide Projector With T.E.V.

Recently teachers have become aware of the value of using a variety of 2 x 2 inch slides in different formats as creative resources to the teaching-learning process. Most churches have available a filmsrtip projector and many of these filmstrip projectors can be adapted for slides with a simple attachment. However, the most satisfactiry way to project slides is with an automatic slide projector. Many members of the church already own slide projectors, which means that someone might be recruited to assist with the class for a couple of weeks and to bring his projector with him.

There are many, many ways to create slides with and without a camera and twice as many ways as that to use them creatively in the classroom. In this chapter we will present several suggestions for creating and using slides to reinforce concepts related to the New Testament.

DO-IT-YOURSELF WRITE-ON SLIDES*

A Write-On slide is a relatively new product manufactured by Eastman Kodak Company. It is just as its name implies — a slide which one can write on with pens or pencils and then show in a slide projector. By the time children are in the second or third grade many of them are already bored with the kinds of materials they are given for creative activities: crayons, construction paper, scissors, and paste. Children today live in a media oriented society. Their experiences are enriched significantly through television. They use all sorts of A-V equipment in school. In order for church education to motivate students to a high level of participation and interest we need to use more interesting materials. Write-On slides are an example of a new resource that students enjoy and can use very creatively.

There are ways that you can use Write-On slides with students in the classroom.

** Because of the transparent element of Write-On slides they can be placed over the line drawings in T.E.V. to trace the lines, thus creating slides with line drawings.

** Students could work in small groups to create visual interpretations of passages of Scripture. Some students could write the script while others draw the slides.

** Instead of seeing a filmstrip of some New Testament person or event the teacher could give the students the script and let them create their own visuals.

** After time spent on a key concept the teacher could give each student one blank Write-On slide on which to create some visual symbol to express the meaning of the key concept. Then all slides could be shown. The slides could be shown with appropriate background music of a song on the same theme, or they could be shown in silence without comment, or there could be a discussion while seeing the slides.

*Write-On Slides are packaged in boxes of 100. They are available from Audio-Visual dealers or GRIGGS EDUCATIONAL SERVICE.

SLIDES FROM BIBLE LANDS

In many congregations there are persons who have traveled abroad and visited the Holy Land. Usually these persons are more than willing to share any slides they may have taken. These same persons may be willing to assist the teacher for several sessions to use their slides with a small group in a creative way. Slides could be selected that show places and objects that are mentioned in the New Testament. Then the students could search for an appropriate passage of Scripture to accompany the slide. A series of slides could be put together that would communicate some very important concepts.

There is another way to arrange for slides of New Testament subjects. A person with a Single Lens Reflex 35 mm camera, with close-up capability, could make a series of slides by copying from photographs, maps, and diagrams that already appear in Atlases and other books. These photographs enhance the message of the books, but they also have the potential of being used by students in the slide format. All that is required is to locate someone with the right camera, then select photographs, diagrams, and maps to photograph. (They need not be torn out of the book they are in.) Give them to your photographer friend and in less than a week you will have a very valuable set of slides that can be used in creative ways.

ILLUSTRATE SCRIPTURE WITH SLIDES

Using a Single Lens Reflex 35 mm Camera, as described above, it is possible to make slides from magazine photographs, ads, and headlines. After I collected about 200 slides of a wide variety of subjects I found that I had an invaluable resource for illustrating passages of Scriptures. I have used my collection of slides in several ways:

	**	Let a small group of students use the slides together to illustrate a parable or some other passage and then share it with the whole group.

	**	Give each student in the class a dozen slides. Read the passage slowly one line at a time so that students can look at their slides to see if any of them are appropriate for the line that is read. When a student selects a slide the teacher, or a student helper, takes the slide and puts it in the slide tray or cartridge. When finished reading, there should be a series of slides that illustrate the whole passage. Then, read the passage again and advance slides in sequence to match what is being read.

** Another way similar to the one above is to give each student an assignment of one or more verses to work on individually with his dozen slides.

** The students could look carefully at their dozen or so slides, group three or four of them into one theme and then search through T.E.V. to find a verse or passage that expresses in words what the slides express visually.

When students select slides to illustrate particular passages of Scripture they not only facilitate a visual expression of the printed word, but they also accomplish several other important things in the learning process. By using contemporary visual images there is an updating of biblical material that is two thousand years old. This makes Scripture as contemporary as last week's magazine. Once when illustrating the Parable of the Lost Son with slides a student said, "I never looked at it that way before. I don't think I will ever forget that parable." Visual expressions of printed materials provide new insights in a way that just reading cannot accomplish.

PHOTOGRAPH THE LINE DRAWINGS

By using Scripture Cards or cut out, mounted line drawings from T.E.V. it is possible to create a set of slides that could be used in worship or instructional settings. Even if you do not own a Single Lens Reflex 35mm camera you probably know someone who does. Recruit that person to work with you on your project. For the price of several rolls of film and some time, you could produce some resources that could be used by you and others for years to come. When the Scripture Cards are photographed and reproduced into color slides they present a beautiful image when projected on a screen or light colored wall. Try it!

Use the Filmstrip Projector With T.E.V.

** Introduction

** Parable of the Lost Son

** Students Write Their Own Script

** Do-It-Yourself Write-On Filmstrip

** Use Filmstrip for Discussion

Thirteen: Use The Filmstrip Projector With T.E.V.

Most churches have available one or more filmstrip projectors. There was a day when filmstrips were used just about every week in some classes. It is true that a lot of filmstrips featuring Bible subjects are of poor quality both in script and photography or art work. However, there are some sources of excellent resources that would provide enough filmstrips to cover most of the major biblical persons and events.

When I announced a workshop on "Creative Uses of Filmstrips" someone said, "I can't think of anything less creative than a filmstrip." I can understand what that person meant if he was basing his judgment upon the ways filmstrips have often been used. I suspect that the following comments of teachers illustrate some misuses of filmstrips.

- "I don't know whether I know enough about the Apostle Paul to teach next Sunday. I wonder if I can find a filmstrip that will cover the subject?"

- "Gee, I don't have enough time to prepare for my class on Sunday, but I'll just pick up a filmstrip at church in the morning."

"The children have been getting restless lately, maybe I better change the pace with a filmstrip."

These are the wrong reasons for using a filmstrip. To be used effectively, a filmstrip should be previewed carefully and chosen for what it can contribute to the overall strategy a teacher has develepod for a particular session.

There are several ways to use filmstrips to help translate some parts of Scripture.

PARABLE OF THE LOST SON

This is a simulated activity designed to help the students identify with the actions and feelings of each of the three main characters in the parable. This activity could be used as part of a larger unit on the parables as a whole. Prior to doing what is suggested here the students will have dealt with "parable" as a form of teaching and writing and they will have had some experience trying to interpret several parables.

Step 1   Teacher could begin with an introduction something like: "We are going to spend a few minutes focusing on the Parable of the Lost Son. There are three main characters: a father, a younger son who leaves home, and an older son who remains home. We are going to see a filmstrip of that parable and each of us is going to look at the filmstrip through the eyes of one of the characters in the parable. Decide which of the three persons you want to identify with. (Allow a few seconds for the students to make a choice and check out to see who has selected which role. It helps if there is a fairly equal distribution of the three roles among the students.) As you see the filmstrip through the eyes of your person there are two questions to think about:

(1) "How do you feel about what is happening to you?"

(2) "How do you feel about the other two persons?"

(It may be helpful to have these questions printed so that the students can see them.)

"Let's see the filmstrip."

Step 2 Show the filmstrip. The one I like to use is "The Loving Father," which is one of a series in *The Parables Jesus Told* produced by Roa's Films. (See Bibliography.) When I show the filmstrip I do not use the recorded script with it. Instead I use the cassette tape of T.E.V. by the American Bible Society and play Luke 15:11-32. It is amazing how well coordinated the frames of the filmstrip are with the biblical text. With a little practice it is very easy to synchronize the filmstrip with the text.

Step 3 After seeing the filmstrip, direct the students to group themselves according to the three roles so that all the "fathers" meet and discuss together as do all the "younger sons" and "older sons." Spend five to ten mininutes in these groups discussing the two questions that were assigned.

Step 4 Reorganize the class by having the students meet in "family groups" which means that one or more persons representing each of the three roles will be gathered together. Again, in these new groups the students share the feelings they have in response to the questions they discussed previously. Usually most of the students have so identified with their role that they move into a dynamic role-playing situation in these "family groups." Ten to fifteen minutes should be sufficient for this step.

Step 5 At this time I usually focus the attention of the whole class in a brief discussion which may include some of these questions:

- What did you learn about your person?

- What did you learn from the other persons?

- Why do you think Jesus told this parable?

- What was Jesus trying to teach about God?

- What are some experiences you know of that are similar to this parable?

(If there is enough time it may be possible to do a creative activity which would include slides, photographs, paints, clay or some other medium.)

Step 6 As a conclusion to the activity I instruct the students to complete the sentence, "God's love is . . . ." Allow one or two minutes for students to think of or write down a completion of the phrase. Then use the statements as part of a litany. Students could speak their statements and as a whole group could respond, "Help us, God, to share your love with others."

There are some very basic principles involved in the above activity which can be incorporated in other activities.

- ** The students have a reason for seeing the filmstrip. There is something to look for and think about while seeing it. This increases the motivation of the student to participate. In this way the filmstrip is not just a "filler," but rather a necessary component to the teaching strategy.

- ** The students had opportunity to make several choices in the session. When students can choose what they will do they will be more motivated to participate.

- ** A variety of activities were used to focus on one main subject. Each activity required involvement by the students. They worked as a whole group, in small groups and by themselves.

- ** The teacher sets the stage for the learning but does not *tell* the students what they should think. The teacher serves in the role of guide and what the students learn they learn because of their own involvement.

- ** A simulated activity (the role identification) involves the students in identifying with the actions and feelings of the characters in the parable. This is a much more powerful activity than just hearing the Scripture and seeing the filmstrip.

- ** The parable is made relevant because it is approached at the feeling level instead of just learning about what happened, where, when, who, etc. The Scriptures will remain two thousand years old if we only focus on the facts, but when we focus on the feelings they become as contemporary as *now*.

STUDENTS WRITE THEIR OWN SCRIPT

In order to increase the value of filmstrips they need to be used in a variety of creative ways so that students are motivated to become more actively involved in their use. If students are always expected to just sit, look, and listen to filmstrips, then they will become bored and passive.

One way to help students become actively involved with filmstrips is to encourage them to write their own scripts. There is no written or unwritten rule that requires scripts to always be used with their filmstrips. There are several techniques that can be used when planning for students to write their own scripts.

- ** Use a filmstrip that was previously shown. Students will be somewhat familiar with the filmstrip, so that it will be a little easier to write the script.

- ** Select a new filmstrip for students to write an accompanying script. This works well when the visuals of the filmstrip are obvious enough to suggest the persons, actions, and feelings that were intended by the artist and author.

- ** When using filmstrips that focus on New Testament subjects, be sure that copies of T.E.V. are provided so that students can refer to it as they are preparing their script.

- ** Ordinarily the activity of writing a script works best when done by a small group of two to four persons. While one small group is using the filmstrip to write a script, an-

—80—

other group could use the published script to create their own Write-On slides or filmstrip. Then project the newly created filmstrip or slide series and read the newly written script together.

** With a larger group, after they have already seen the filmstrip the teacher could show again a number of selected frames. Show each selected frame for 15-20 seconds. During the brief time the students could write a one-line caption. Continue through the selected frames without comment. After all frames are shown and captions written, show the filmstrip again and this time the students could read their one-line captions for each of the selected frames.

DO-IT-YOURSELF WRITE-ON FILMSTRIP*

With colored projection pens and pencils and twelve to eighteen inches of Write-On filmstrip materials the teachers can provide an inexpensive creative activity for the students to use to express themselves. What was suggested for Write-On slides also applies to Write-On filmstrips.

There are some considerations to make when deciding whether to use Write-On slides or Write-On filmstrips:

- Write-On filmstrip material is less expensixe (about one cent per frame) than Write-On slides (five cents per slide).

- A Write-On slide has four times the amount of writing surface than one frame of Write-On filmstrip.

- When *one student* is working on a sequence of visuals requiring ten or more frames it may be best for him to use Write-On filmstrip material.

- When a *group of students* is working together on one series of visuals, then it is much easier to use the slide format than the filmstrip format.

* Write-On filmstrip material is available in various length from some Audio-Visual Dealers.

- Slides can be used and reused in a variety of ways with different combinations of sequences; whereas the filmstrip format is more rigid. The sequence of frames in a filmstrip is "locked-in" and permanent.

USE FILMSTRIP FOR DISCUSSION

Instead of showing filmstrip with a script, teachers could use the filmstrip as a focus for discussion. With one or more well phrased questions for each frame teachers could guide a discussion of a parable, an event in Jesus' ministry, or some other New Testament subject.

Use the 16mm Projector With T.E.V.

    **   Introduction

    **   Story-Line Films With Annie Vallotton

    **   Some Ways To Use 16mm Films

    **   Four Film Experiences

Fourteen: Use The 16mm Projector With T.E.V.

Films have been used in church education for years. When I was in fifth and sixth grade I went to a Sunday School where once each month a film was shown to all the classes gathered in the social hall. I liked those Sundays because I liked films and did not see too many of them. (Remember, that was prior to television.) It did not make any difference what the quality or subject of the film was, it was always more interesting than going to class.

I suspect we can all recall times when teachers have:

- seen a good film and used it even though it was inappropriate for the lesson;
- used a film as a time filler;
- thought the class needed a little entertainment to change the pace; or
- ordered films from catalogues or on someone else's recommendation.

This misuse of films often confuses leaders about the value of films in teaching. Films for educational settings must be chosen carefully and used creatively.

The medium of film has tremendous potential for achieving many educational objectives. Films can be used to *introduce* a subject. There are many New Testament teachings that are explored in a general way in secular films that can contribute much to a class in the church. Films are an effective means to *motivate* persons to think, feel, or express themselves in areas of personal interest. Films can also be used to *present* another point of view than what is represented by the teachers or students. Many half-hour television programs have been reproduced and are available in 16mm format.

Ordinarily short films (5-20 minutes) are the most useful when the teacher is confronted with a time limit of one hour or less. A film can be an important part of the class period, but should not be the dominant element. Short films have the advantages of being less expensive to rent and they can be shown twice in the same period if desired.

STORY LINE FILMS FEATURING ANNIE VALLOTTON

Story Line Films are a television production of the American Bible Society designed for children of all ages and available in the 16mm format. Annie Vallotton, creator of the T.E.V. line drawings, starts each program describing a key line she will use in her presentation. Presently there are thirteen films; eleven from the Gospels and two from the Old Testament.

Miss Vallotton uses giant panes of glass and colored markers to illustrate her stories in a style that is uniquely hers. You can see her delightful face, as well as her creation as she draws, tells, sings, and even yodels to communicate her message. Annie Vallotton captures the essence of each story in just a few simple lines and words. She is a masterful teacher, story teller, artist and communicator. Each film is just five minutes long. Even though they were designed for children I have found that the child in each of us responds affirmatively to each film.

Cat. No.	Title	Tells About
19101	*The Good Neighbor*	A Samaritan who cared
19102	*Stick By Your Friend*	David, Jonathan, and trouble
19103	*Listening to God*	Some seeds and how they grew
19104	*Show-Off*	A rich man, a widow, and giving
19105	*The Happy Man*	Jesus and the man who couldn't walk but did

19106	*A Baby Named Jesus*	Jesus' birthday
19107	*Runaway Comes Home*	How much a dad loved his dropout son
19108	*Hosanna Day*	Jesus' welcome to Jerusalem
19109	*Conversation*	The pharisee, the publican, and God
19110	*God Loves Us*	The shepherd and his lost-and-found sheep
19111	*It Is Written*	Christ's death and resurrection
19112	*God Protects*	David and the Giant Goliath
19113	*Afraid of the Storm*	A rocking boat, upset disciples, and a calm Jesus

These films can be rented from Association Films or purchased from the American Bible Society. (See Bibliography for addresses.)

There are several ways the films can be used:

* ** A story Line film could be used at the beginning of a session to introduce a biblical story which will be explored further in the class.

* ** The same film could be shown as a summary or review of the biblical story that was studied during the session.

* ** Or, one Story Line film could be shown twice in the same session; first as an introduction, then after a period of discussion and study it could be used for a time of reflection or worship.

* ** In worship services or celebrations the film could be used before or after or instead of the reading of Scripture.

* ** If several media are available (filmstrip, record, song, teaching pictures, etc.) a Story Line film could be used with one or more of the other media as a way to compare interpretations of a biblical subject.

* ** In teacher training the Story Line films could be used as excellent examples of effective teacher presentations in a deductive style.

SOME WAYS TO USE 16mm FILMS

Creative teachers have discovered many, many ways to use films effectively in their teaching strategies. Following are several ways that have proven themselves by many teachers:

* ** *View With A Purpose* — Before showing the film the teacher can state one or more questions for the students to think about while viewing the film. If several questions are stated, the class could be divided into several groups, or students could make a choice of which question to focus on. After seeing the film the students could discuss questions in small groups or as a whole class. Other tasks could be assigned prior to the film, such as looking for specific emphases or making a list in some specific categories. The value of this approach is that persons are much more actively involved in viewing if they have something specific to guide them.

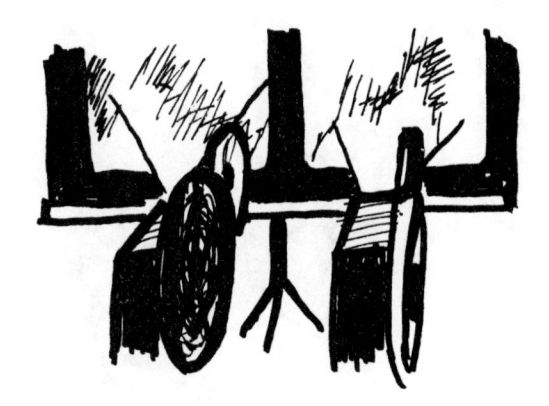

** *Show Contrasting Films* — When using films to introduce a subject or to motivate persons to express themselves creatively there is real value in showing two short films related to the same subject. The films should have different points of view, different cinemagraphic styles or other contrasting characteristics that will provide a basis for comparison and discussion. Usually the two films would be projected separately, but there may be value with some films to project them a second time simultaneously using only one soundtrack or perhaps even a separate recorded song or spoken word.

** *Show A Segment of a Film* — There are no written or unwritten rules that require a person to show the entire film. Some longer films have very valuable, complete-in-themselves, segments that could be used separately. This would be more true of training or documentary types of films than of dramatic films.

** *Stop the Film in the Middle* — Many films that are presenting a narrative or documentation of a theme or event can be stopped at one or more appropriate places in the midst of showing the film. At that point the teacher could:

- Engage the class in a review and discussion of what they have seen to that point.

- Involve the class in discussing what they anticipate might happen and why.

- Leave the lights dimmed and encourage the students to reflect on the feelings of a particular character by speaking in the role of that character, in the first-person singular.

- Lead the students to compare two or more sections of the film as additional information or experience is presented.

** *Show A Film With Another Media* — Persons are very capable of focusing upon more than one media at a time. Use a film without soundtrack and play phonograph record or tape recording as the soundtrack. Films and slides can be projected side by side on the same screen or two screens. Films can be projected on mirrors, ceilings, weather balloons, and walls for added effect.

** *Films and Role-Playing* — Films which present situations involving persons with real concerns can be used to motivate the viewers to identify with those same concerns. *Before* viewing the film persons can be introduced to the character with which they are to identify. *During* the film the viewer focuses on the experiences and feelings of that person. *After* the film discuss the issues in the first-person from the perspective of the character who was selected. If several characters were selected, then it is possible to mix up the characters in small groups.

FOUR FILM EXPERIENCES

For three years I have been associated with Sister Charlene Tschirhart of the Sisters of Social Service. Sister Charlene is what is affectionately known as a "media nut." She loves films and uses films as creatively as anyone I know. Sister Charlene has written several outlines of teaching activities or experiences teachers could plan for their students. My thanks to Sister Charlene for what follows.

1. "Let the children come to me because . . . "Unless you become like a child you cannot enter the kingdom." Because . . . children dream and fantasize.

   To dream is to understand . . . to dream is to contemplate human situations and to see more deeply into the meaning and significance of life.

   - *Pass out Scripture Card* illustrating Matthew 19:13-15 with the title, "Let the Children Come," (order No. 06722, from the American Bible Society). *Look* at the drawing, notice what the characters are doing, read the Scripture on the reverse side. (Perhaps read in unison.) *Divide into small groups* to discuss: What do you think Jesus meant when he said, "Let the children come to me . . . because the kingdom of heaven belongs to such as these." Spend five to ten minutes in small groups, then share in small groups.

   - *Emphasize* that children dream and fantasize. Relate this to the experience of contemplation — to be able to see deeper meanings. *Listen* to the recording of *The Sounds of Love*. (Available from the Franciscan Communications Center, 1229 South Santee St., Los Angeles, CA 90015.) *Listen* to the first band (60 seconds), then play it over again. *Ask* participants to notice how the child is aware of deeper meanings. Elicit comments on the child's ability to dream.

   - *Ask* each person to write in his own words a completion of the sentence, "Let the children come to me because . . ."

   - *Show* the telespot "Sleepy World," one minute, color, 16mm, also available from Franciscan Communications Center. *Invite* persons to read their complete statements. Play the last band of the record, "Love, Like a Kid Again."

2. *DAISY* — 6 minute color animation rental. Available from Mass Media, 2116 North Charles St., Baltimore, MD 21218.

   "If I had my life to live over I'd pick more daisies."

The central character, a Daisy, is a delightful image of beauty and goodness. As the flower sprouts from the earth a man hurries to uproot the small plant. The flower remains firmly in place while the man's anger and frustration increases. Then a child appears, finds delight in Daisy, and with a gentle touch the child plucks the flower.

Some questions to consider after viewing the film:

- Who does the man represent? Why did he want to pick the flower?

- Who does the child represent? Why did he want to pick the flower?

- With whom did you identify? Why?

- Compare the flower's action to the way people relate.

- Jesus said, "The meek shall inherit the earth." Could this be a subtitle for the movie? Why? Why not?

- What other subtitle would you give this film?

Daisy could be used effectively with any church group regardless of age. Try giving everyone a daisy as they arrive. Encourage them to look at their daisy and reflect on what they see and are reminded of.

Daisy could be used in a family worship setting, children's program, high school group or perhaps for teacher training.

A brief, powerful word about reaching toward and relating to other people.

3. *THE STRAY* — 16mm, color, 14 minutes, rental from Franciscan Communications Center, 1229 South Santee Street, Los Angeles, CA 90015.

Have you seen any lost sheep lately? . . . Most of us will answer "no"! However, after we see *The Stray* we will remember many times when we lost someone or were lost ourselves. *The Stray* is a film experience designed for the young and the young at heart and translates the Parable of the Lost Sheep in a beautiful and powerful way. In this story there are twelve active, wide-eyed children (sheep) accompanied to the zoo by a loveable, harried bus driver (shepherd). The stray is a little boy identified by, "I'm a tiger number 12." The interaction of bus driver, children, and animals transforms the Scriptural tale into a contemporary adventure full of fun and fantasy, illumined by the ageless truth of God's love.

The Stray can be used in many ways . . .

   . . . . in the classroom — to communicate the meaning of the Parable of the Lost Sheep (Matthew 18:12-14 and Luke 15:3.)

   . . . . as a prayer experience — read parable from the Bible, have persons imagine the story as they hear it. Show film and think about feelings of being lost and being found. Share parable, film, and feelings. Encourage prayers of petition and thanksgiving. Conclude with singing, reciting, or reading Psalm 23, "The Lord is my shepherd. . . ."

. . . . for teacher training — think of the bus driver as a teacher. Look for the actions and attitudes of a creative teacher. Show film again looking for all the learnings of the children.

4. *CLOWN* — 16mm, color, 15 minutes, rental from Learning Corporation of America, 711 Fifth Avenue, New York, N. Y. 10022.

Have you seen any clowns lately?

Clown is a poetic movie about a shaggy dog and a little boy. The two are inseparable. One day as the boy is playing with other boys Clown wanders away and becomes lost. The boy searches desperately for his friend. When he is about to give up, Clown is seen peering around the corner of a building. With joy and excitement the two meet. Soon after the boy's face becomes very serious as he discovers that his pet is now a guide dog for a blind man. After a moment of reflection the boy decides to quietly slip away and leave his beloved Clown to the blind man. This film without words will be a delight to all ages and can be used in a wide variety of ways. The film artistically develops the concepts of companionship, loss, gift-giving, sacrifice, and sympathy.

Clown could be used for:

- family worship service or time of fellowship;

- a teaching session in religious education class;

- training programs for teacher; and

- an introduction to Lent.

Before viewing the film ask everyone to recall a time when they lost something or were separated from someone they treasured very much. After everyone has shared their recollections show *Clown*. Then, encourage the group to give their immediate reactions. Some questions to consider: Why did the boy give up (sacrifice) his dog? What was the boy's feeling(s) as he left Clown with the blind man?

Use the Thermal Copier

AND SPIRIT DUPLICATOR WITH T.E.V.

** Introduction

** Make Thermal Transparencies

** Make Thermal Spirit Masters

** Prepare Student Worksheets

** Reproduce Student Creativity

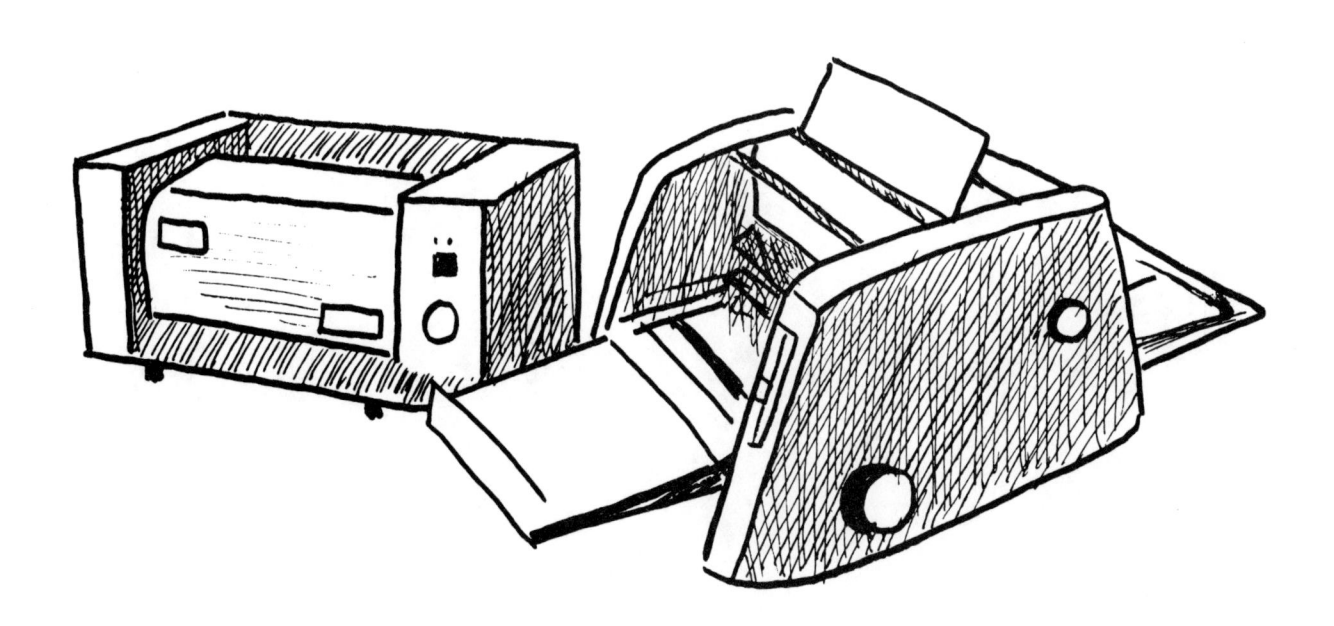

Fifteen: Use Thermal Copier and Spirit Duplicator With T.E.V.

All churches have some means of duplication for church newsletters, bulletins and other printed materials. Usually mimeograph or offset duplicating machines are used because they provide good quality printing in black or other colors. Whenever teachers want materials reproduced in quantity for use by the class there is a hesitation to have them mimeographed because of the time and cost involved. It usually means asking the church secretary or someone else to type the stencil and run off the copies on the mimeograph. Because of the problems involved, most teachers do not often prepare materials to be duplicated for classroom use.

There is a way to provide teachers with the means to duplicate materials for classroom use. A *Spirit Duplicating Machine* (often referred to as a Ditto machine, which is one of the more familiar brands) provides an easy-to-use, inexpensive way for teachers and students to duplicate materials. A spirit duplicator uses spirit masters from which to make copies. A spirit master consists of a white front sheet and a carbon backing sheet, separated by a protective sheet of tissue paper. The typing, writing or drawing is done directly on the white front sheet after the tissue paper has been removed. One can type directly on the white front sheet or use a ballpoint pen to print or draw on it. Spirit masters usually print in purple, but other colors are available and provide more versatility in visual compositions. You can even duplicate something in several colors by creating the master in several stages.

A basic spirit duplicator is a very easy machine to operate. All teachers on a staff could be instructed quickly on how to create masters and operate the machine. I personally believe that teachers should have access to such equipment. Even if a church does not own one, it may be possible to make arrangements with another church in town or a local school to use theirs on occasion. I wanted a spirit duplicator for my own personal use, so I checked with a local office machines store to see if any used, reconditioned machines were available. One was not available at the time, but they said they would call me when one came in. Within three weeks I had a spirit duplicator for which I paid only $75.00. It is hand-operated and works as good as a new one.

Another piece of office equipment which is nice to have available is a *Thermal Copying Machine*. Sometimes a thermal copier is identified as a thermofax machine or an infrared transparency maker. Doctors and dentists often use thermal copiers to do their billing. Most schools have at least one thermal copier in the teachers' workroom or office. A thermal copier reproduces typewritten, printed, or other faxible copy on paper, spirit master, or overhead transparencies. The primary requirement for reproducing something on a thermal copier is that the ink or lead of the original have a carbon base such as lead pencil, offset reproducing pencils and pens, typewriter ribbon, newspaper ink, mimeograph ink, offset ink and some marking pens. A thermal copier costs more than $250.00 new, but it is possible to find used machines for much less. Generally speaking, a used thermal copier that has been reconditioned will serve very well for whatever use will be made of it in the church.

If teachers have available a spirit duplicator and/or a thermal copier there are a variety of things they can do with them to increase their resourcefulness.

MAKE THERMAL TRANSPARENCIES

If a church has an overhead projector and a thermal copier it is possible to reproduce transparencies for many uses. Teachers may want to use any of the following items as originals from which to make transparency:

- cartoons or comic strips
- headlines or captions from magazines or newspapers
- large print sections of T.E.V.
- line drawings from T.E.V.
- typewritten materials (Do not use standard typewriter size of type; it is too small when projected. Use a primary type typewriter which may be borrowed from an elementary teacher in the primary grades.)
- maps such as the ones included in this book
- diagrams, designs, symbols or other illustrations prepared by the teacher
- graphs, charts, or outlines
- student-created materials (Be sure to use proper pens and pencils.)

In order to make a thermal transparency it is necessary to have the proper transparency material. All audio-visual dealers that handle supplies for the overhead projector will have available material that can be used in a thermal copier to make transparencies. (See Bibliography for several direct sources.)

The way to make a transparency is:

1. Select a bold-line, dark print, carbon-based original.
2. Place thermal transparency on top of the original with notched corner on the upper right.
3. Insert both original and thermal transparency directly into the thermal copier or into a carrier, then into the machine.
4. With thermal copier set at the proper temperature you will have in seconds a beautifully prepared transparency.

Thermal transparency sheets cost between 15 and 25 cents each for clear, black-line sheets and between 25 and 30 cents for color, black-line sheets. This is an expensive material but when a transparency is made it is permanent and can be used over and over again without any loss of quality.

MAKE THERMAL SPIRIT MASTERS

When you have access to both a thermal copier and a spirit duplicating machine it is possible to make spirit masters from the same originals as suggested in the previous section. Office supply stores, school supply stores, or audio-visual dealers will stock thermal spirit masters. When you have such masters they can be inserted, with the original faxible copy, into the thermal copier and in seconds you will have available a spirit master to run off up to 150 copies that will be reproductions of the original.

There is a material available that will allow you to make a spirit master and thermal transparency with the same item. What this means is that the master is made on a clear plastic sheet which serves both as a transparency and spirit master. My experience with this material is that you end up with a poor quality transparency and a poor quality spirit master. I prefer to take a little extra time and spend a little more to end up with good quality transparency and spirit master by doing them in separate steps using different material for each.

PREPARE STUDENT WORKSHEETS

In other chapters of this book we have suggested several values to preparing worksheets for students to use:

> ** It is helpful for students to have in visual, printed form all the instructions they need to complete a specific project or assignment.
>
> ** When students have worksheets to use they can work at their own pace without depending upon the teacher to direct them in every step.
>
> ** It is possible for students to work individually or in small groups on different projects when each has his own printed guidelines.
>
> ** Master teachers can prepare ahead of time many worksheets to be used by several classes that are supervised by less experienced teachers.
>
> ** A lot of materials such as data, questions, Scripture references, definitions, maps, charts, etc., can be included on the worksheets, thus saving teachers from having to present it all verbally and then having to repeat it many times because students did not remember.

Worksheets for students to use can be prepared with typewriter, or by hand with ballpoint pen, on a spirit master. This can be done at home, then run off at church in a matter of seconds and be available for use in the classroom. Be sure to save the spirit masters that are prepared. They should be catalogued and filed so they will be available for other teachers to use at another time.

REPRODUCE STUDENT CREATIVITY

When students are motivated effectively they are often inspired to create beautiful statements and expressions of what they think and feel through words or drawings. Teachers can reinforce individual students by showing appreciation and pleasure for what they have created and commenting positively about what they have done. This reinforcement is necessary in order to encourage students to continue to be creative. Another way to reinforce students and to share with others their creativity is to reproduce it so that others may have copies. Recently I received from a teacher spirit copies of cinquain and haiku poems that fifth and sixth graders had created. The students had written a lot of poems and each student was encouraged to select one or two of his own poems that were his favorites or the ones he felt best expressed the concepts they had focused on. As a result the students selected about thirty different poems that the teacher typed on a spirit master and duplicated on the spirit duplicator. Not only did each student receive a copy of the poems he and his fellow students had created, but copies were shared with others in the church.

One of the problems of church education is its low profile or lack of visibility among the members of the church. Also, seldom do teachers and students in one class know what is happening in another class. By reproducing student creativity on spirit masters and duplicating copies to be shared with others it is possible to increase awareness, interest and support by others as well as communicate much insight about biblical subjects as understood by students in the church.

A class could focus on a time in Jesus' life or in the life of the early church. After some research and with a little imagination the students could create a two or three page newspaper which would express in a creative form ways the students interpret those events. This newspaper could be reproduced with a spirit duplicator.

Bibliography

** American Bible Society Resources

** Resource Books for Teachers

** Books to Use for Classroom Study With Students

** Resources for Values Clarification

** Cassette Recording Resources

** Filmstrip Resources

** Addresses of Sources for Educational Resources

** Audio-Visual Materials

Bibliography

See Sources of Resources section for addresses of all publishers, suppliers, etc., listed in this Bibliography.

AMERICAN BIBLE SOCIETY RESOURCES

In addition to the resources mentioned in this book, the American Bible Society has many other resources that are inexpensive and very useful for teaching in the church. In what follows there will be a representative listing of ABS resources with order number and cost as of June, 1973.

1. *T.E.V. New Testaments*

# 02790	Regular Edition (paperback)	$ .40
# 02820	Imprimatur Edition (paperback)	.40
# 02799	Regular Edition (hardback, vinyl cover)	1.00
# 02836	Regular Edition plus Psalms (paperback)	.50
# 02850	Large Print Edition	1.50

2. *T.E.V. New Testament Portions*

    - Matthew, Mark, Luke, John, Acts with line drawings. .... .07 each
    - Large Print Portions, Matthew, Mark, Luke, John, Acts, Psalms. .... .25 each

3. *T.E.V. Complete New Testament on fifteen cassette tapes in* attractive, durable album

    #14015 .... $30.75

4. *Chart of the English Bible,* the development of Scriptures from 40 A.D. to the present. Concise pertinent data on each translation is given on the back, #15010, in units of 100.... $1.25

5. *Our Most Precious Heritage,* a full-color, 32 page picture booklet describing how our heritage came to us, #15020 .... $ .20

6. *Love Posters,* five 18 x 20 inch posters in vivid colors proclaiming the biblical concept of love, #15627 .... $3.25

7. *Joy Posters,* five 18 x 30 inch posters in vivid colors focusing on the concept of joy, #17094 .... $3.25

8. *Teaching Posters of the Bible Around the World*

    Sixteen four color posters each showing Matthew 5:7-8 in a different language with a picture of people who speak that language in their cultural setting. Each set of posters has a plastic, long-play record by which the verses can be heard being spoken in the various languages. A teacher's guide includes a story to accompany each translation. This is one of the finest resources available for helping students identify with the fact of the Bible being a special book for all people of the world. # 15014 .... $1.50

9. *Twelve Scripture Posters,* selected line drawings by Annie Vallotton, from T.E.V. 16 x 22 inches, #15052 .... $2.00

RESOURCE BOOKS FOR TEACHERS

There are many, many books published which would be of help to teachers as they prepare for teaching. The books listed below are the ones that I personally use. Check the church library and talk with your pastor about books he has in his library which you may be able to borrow. Most of these books could be ordered through any local bookstore.

1. COMPANION TO THE NEW TESTAMENT, A.E. Harvey; Oxford University Press, 1970.
    This book is similar to a commentary. The biblical text which provides the basis for the book in The New English Bible New Testament.

2. CONCISE CONCORDANCE, Revised Standard Version, Thomas Nelson and Sons, 1959.

   An excellent small concordance for teachers and students to use.

3. THE COTTON PATCH VERSION OF LUKE AND ACTS by Clarence Jordan; Associaton Press, 1969.

   A modern translation with a Southern accent; fervent, earthy, rich in humor, by a dramatic, courageous Baptist pastor.

4. THE DAILY STUDY BIBLE by William Barclay; Westminster Press, 1959.
   In sixteen volumes Dr. Barclay provides a very easy to read and understand commentary and interpretation of all the New Testament books.

5. GREAT PERSONALITIES OF THE NEW TESTAMENT: THEIR LIVES AND TIMES by William Sanford Le Soc; Revell Company, 1961.

   Seventeen of the major personalities of the New Testament are presented in a way that helps the reader sort out the isolated Scripture verses and put them together in an understandable whole.

6. HARPER'S BIBLE DICTIONARY by Madeleine S. Miller and J. Lane Miller; Harper and Brothers Publishers, 1954.

   One of the best, most readable one-volume Bible Dictionaries. Can also be used by older students.

7. INTERPRETER'S ONE-VOLUME COMMENTARY ON THE BIBLE, ed. by Charles M. Laymon; Abingdon Press, 1971.

   A completely new 1,424 page commentary is not a condensation of *The Interpreter's Bible*. Seventy scholars contributed to the general articles and comments. Contains 140 photographs. Oriented to a broad readership of laymen, students and ministers.

8. JESUS AS THEY SAW HIM by William Barrclay; Harper and Row, publishers, 1962.

   In this book Dr. Barclay surveys the many ways Jesus is presented and interpreted by others in the New Testament.

9. LAND OF CHRIST by Andre Parrot; Fortress Press, 1968.

   A beautiful blend of archaeology, history, and geography presenting the life of Jesus in chronological order with related Scripture texts and appropriate photographs.

10. PAUL — ENVOY EXTRAORDINARY by Malcolm Muggeridge and Alec Vidler; Harper and Row, Publishers, 1972.

    This is a very unique book based on a television series by BBC. It is written in dialogue form and is illustrated with beautiful color photographs.

11. THE TWELVE CHRIST CHOSE by Asbury Smith; Harper and Brothers, 1958.

    A popularly written, easy to read overview of each of the twelve apostles.

12. UNDERSTANDING THE NEW TESTAMENT by Howard Clark Kee and Franklin W. Young; Pretice-Hall, Inc., 1958.

    An excellent scholarly overview of New Testament content, history, problems, etc., based upon careful research and useful as a reference book for teachers and adult students of the Bible.

BOOKS TO USE FOR CLASSROOM STUDY WITH STUDENTS

1. BIBLE ENCYCLOPEDIA FOR CHILDREN by Cecil Northcott; The Westminster Press, Philadelphia, 1964.

   This book is very similar to a Bible Dictionary for children. Illustrated with drawings in color and Bible references for each word.

2. DISCOVERING THE BIBLE by G.W.H. Lampe and David Scott Daniel; Abingdon Press, 1966.

An excellent book for young students. Two sections: the first with stories about the Bible and the second a reference section with facts about the Bible.

3. GOLDEN BIBLE ATLAS by Samuel Terrien; Golden Press, New York, 1964.

4. KNOW YOUR BIBLE by Mary Alice Jones; Rand McNally and Company, New York, 1967.

   This is a very good introduction to basic facts and information about the origin and devlopment of the Bible. This would be an invaluable book for use by junior and junior high students.

5. LIFE IN BIBLE TIMES by Robert Henderson and Ian Gould; Rand McNally and Company, New York, 1967.

   With a clear, simple text and very helpful illustrations this book provides an introduction to children of the style of life of people in Bible times.

6. PEOPLE OF THE BIBLE by Cecil Northcutt; The Westminster Press, Philadelphia, 1967.

   By the same author of BIBLE ENCYCLOPEDIA FOR CHILDREN, this book provides a very succinct introduction to many of the key persons of the Bible.

7. YOUNG PEOPLE'S BIBLE DICTIONARY by Barbara Smith; The Westminster Press, Philadelphia, 1965.

   Many of the words of the Bible are explained with very clear and short definitions. Included are several key Scripture references for each word.

8. YOUNG READERS DICTIONARY OF THE BIBLE, Abingdon Press, 1969.

   Many key words defined with colorful illustrations and Scriptural references.

9. YOUNG READERS BOOK OF BIBLE STORIES by Helen Doss, illustrated by Tom Armstrong; Abingdon Press, 1970.

   Many Bible characters and their surroundings are presented as being as real as today's headlines. Includes Bible references for each story.

RESOURCES FOR VALUES CLARIFICATION

1. TWO BOOKS

   Values and Teaching

   Raths, Harmin, and Simon
   Charles E. Merrill Publishing Company

   Values Clarification

   A handbook of practical strategies for teachers and students.

   Simon, Howe, and Kirschenbaum
   Hart Publishing Company

These two books are indispensible to anyone seeking to understand and implement the values clarification approach to teaching values.

Values and Teaching is the first book which contains the background of the development and rationale for the approach. It also includes a variety of strategies. *The Values Clarification* book is a collection of seventy-nine different strategies that have been used with elementary and secondary students in classrooms.

2. *A FILM*

   Values Systems Techniques

   16mm, 28min., black and white. Purchase or rental.
   Available from:

   > Executive Secretary for A-V
   > Executive Council for the Episcopal Church
   > 815 Second Avenue, New York, N.Y. 10017

Features Dr. Sidney Simon conducting five different values clarification strategies. The film was produced by the Episcopal Church in a live workshop setting where Dr. Simon was demonstrating for a large group of adults his techniques with six senior high students.

Even though the technical quality of the film does not meet high professional standards, I found the film exceptionally helpful in introducing teachers to Dr Simon and his approaches to value clarification. The six students Dr. Simon works with are very cooperative and candid in their responses and it seems that a perceptive, creative teacher with this introduction could be very effective in leading students in some value clarification strategies.

The five strategies presented in this film are Voting, Rank Order, Value Continuum, Proud Line, and Personal Interview. Not only are the five strategies presented clearly, it is very helpful to observe Dr. Simon's style, approach, and point of view.

I have used *Value Systems Techniques* in several different workshops with church teachers from grade five through adult classes. I do not show the entire film in one sitting. I show one section (or strategy) at a time. After viewing Dr. Simon using the strategy I involve the workshop participants in experiencing the same strategy.

3. *A GAME*

   Values — a board game in box.

   Available from:
   > Friendship Press
   > P.O. Box 37844
   > Cincinnati, Ohio 45237

Very good game to use with four to six persons of junior high age or older. Could be used effectively with adults also. The win - lose aspect of the game is very low-key and depending upon the approach of the teacher could be ignored. The game is essentially a means for involving persons in verbally expressing themselves concerning their personally held values. Depending upon the luck of the spinner, a player may be expected to speak on a value for one or two minutes, may be interviewed by the other players for three minutes, or may be asked one question by each of the other players. There are five stacks of cards with a wide variety of situations and subjects to which the players will respond by expressing their values.

4. *A TEACHER EDUCATION DESIGN* ..

   A Workshop on Value Clarification

   Parish Teacher/Leader Training Unit 8, prepared by the
   Executive Council of the Episcopal Church. 47 pages.

   Available from:
   > Seabury Press
   > 815 Second Avenue
   > New York, N.Y. 10017

This manual is designed to serve as an outline for a person or group planning to conduct a values clarification workshop. The workshop is planned for five 2½ hour sessions with the following emphases: A Theory of Valuing, The Values Gap, Leadership for Values Clarification, Values and Value Indicators, and Implications. Each session includes several different values clarification strategies with opportunity for participants to experience directly many of the strategies.

I would recommend this manual for anyone who wants to develop a workshop for teachers and leaders in the church on the subject of values clarification.

CASSETTE RECORDING RESOURCES

1. American Bible Society cassette tapes with recording of the complete T.E.V. Fifteen cassettes

2. Argus Communications has published many sets of cassette tapes on a wide variety of subjects. One set appropriate to the focus of this book is ENJOYING THE NEW TESTAMENT by Father George Montague. The set includes four cassettes.

3. Avant Garde Records has produced many phonograph records by outstanding religious recording artists. Some are also available on cassette tapes which include "Joy Is Like the Rain," "I Know the Secret," "Knock, Knock," "Keep the Rumor Going," "Go Tell Everyone," "Follow Me," "Busy Day," and "Mass of a Pilgrim People."

4. *Switched On Scripture* (SOS) by Dennis Benson includes a series of C-60 cassette tapes and leader's guides for a six-week session program. Published by Abingdon Press.

5. Thesis Tapes has produced a series of cassette tapes by the title of *Faith Alive*. The following focus on New Testament subjects in a very dramatic way:

    Cassette III - 1   Childhood and Beginning of Jesus' ministry

    Cassette III - 2   Jesus Calls the Disciples

    Cassette IV - 1   Palm Sunday, The Trial, The Crucifixion, The Resurrection

    Cassette IV - 2   After the Resurrection: Matthias, Peter, Stephen, Philip

    Cassette V - 1   Paul: Damascus Road, Escape, Barnabas, Philippian Jailer

    Cassette V - 2   Paul: Mars Hill, a Secret Plot, Shipwreck, at home

FILMSTRIP RESOURCES

1. *Graded Press, United Methodist Church*

    There are many filmstrips produced to accompany Graded Press Curriculum but which would serve as excellent resources for churches using other curriculum.

    - "Into All the World," Part 1, 34 frames with cassette recording
    - "Into All the World," Part 2, 32 frames with cassette recording.

    Very contemporary art with good script provides excellent overview of New Testament themes, events, and persons.

2. *Thomas S. Klise Company* has produced 92 sets of very creative filmstrips. The style of art work and narrative text is very contemporary. Several sets are appropriate to our focus on New Testament studies:
    - "The Man for Others," four filmstrips, two records, approximately 40 frames per filmstrip, presents an overview of the life, teachings and theological significance of Jesus Christ.

    - "Images of Christ," eight filmstrips, four records, each filmstrip approximately 50 frames and 10 minutes in length. Intended for high school students and older.

3. *Pflaum/Standard Publishers* are the producers of Little People's Paperback series of books and filmstrips. A series, PARABLES, includes the Little Grain of Wheat, The Good Samaritan, The King and the Servant, The Prodigal Son, The Great Harvest, and The Generous Vinegrower. Nineteen frames for each filmstrip with script (no record).

4. *Roa's Films* has produced three sets of filmstrips on New Testament Subjects.
    - "The Parables of the Kingdom," eight filmstrips present ten parables of Jesus with 33⅓ recordings.

- "Paul and the Early Church," eight filmstrips and recordings present overview of apostles and early church with emphasis on Paul.

- "My Name Is Jesus," a new production of ten filmstrips on the life and ministry of Jesus. Ten filmstrips and recordings of script written in the first person.

5. *United Church of Christ Filmstrips* includes the following titles:

    - "A.D. 29," 50 frames, script for adults and children, no recording. Focus on the days between Jesus' crucifixion and resurrection.

    - "Five Parables of Jesus," 63 frames, with record and guide, 10 minutes, presents five parables of Jesus: The Sower, The Good Samaritan, The Lost Sheep, The Talents and The Prodigal Son. Each parable could be used separately.

    - "What Do We See of Jesus," two-part color filmstrip with separate scripts for children and adults. The story of Jesus shown through many great works of art.

    - "Why We Celebrate Holy Week," 56 frames with recording present outstanding visuals of persons and events related to Jesus' last week, from triumphant entry to resurrection.

Addresses of Sources for Educational Resources

AMERICAN BIBLE SOCIETY

P.O. Box 5656
Grand Central Station
New York, N.Y. 10017

Good News for Modern Man resources
cassette tapes, picture sets
Free catalogue

ARGUS COMMUNICATIONS

7440 North Natchez Avenue
Niles, Illinois 60648

Cassette tapes, filmstrips,
posters, teacher training kits,
free catalogue

ASSOCIATION FILMS (Regional Libraries)

25358 Cypress Avenue
Hayward, California 94544

6420 West Lake Street
Minneapolis, Minnesota 55426

2221 So. Olive Street
Los Angeles, California 90007

600 Grand Avenue
Ridgefield, New Jersey 07657

5797 New Peachtree Road
Atlanta, Georgia 30340

915 N.W. 19th Avenue
Portland, Oregon 97209

512 Burlington Avenue
La Grange, Illinois 60525

324 Deleward Avenue
Oakmont, Pennsylvania 15139

484 King Street
Littleton, Massachusetts 01460

8615 Directors Row
Dallas, Texas 75247

AVANT GARDE REECORDS

250 West 57th Street
New York, N.Y. 10019

Phonograph records, cassette tapes,
free catalogue

COKESBURY BOOKSTORES REGIONAL SERVICE CENTERS

1600 Queen Anne Road
Teaneck, New Jersey 07666

1910 Main Street
Dallas, Texas 75221

Fifth and Grace Streets
Richmond, Virginia 23261

1635 Adrian Rd.
Burlingame, California 94010

201 Eighth Avenue, South
Nashville, Tennessee 37202

Graded Press filmstrips
Switched On Scripture cassettes
curriculum resources
Bible resource books
free catalogue

1661 North Northwest Hwy.
Park Ridge, Illinois 60068

FRIENDSHIP PRESS

Distribution Office
P.O. Box 37844
Cincinnati, Ohio 45237

Maps, posters, prints, photographs,
filmstrips, records, simulation games, and
books related to the mission of the church.
Free catalogue.

GRIGGS EDUCATIONAL SERVICE

1731 Barcelona St.
Livermore, California 94550

Books, simulations, Scripture Cards,
media resources. Free catalogue.

THOMAS S. KLISE COMPANY

P.O. Box 3418
Peoria, Illinois 61614

Several sets of filmstrips on New
Testament subjects. Free catalogue.

PFLAUM/STANDARD PUBLISHING

    38 West Fifth Street
    Dayton, Ohio 45402

Little People paperback books and filmstrips, picture-poster sets. Free catalogue.

ROA'S FILMS

    1696 North Astor Street
    Milwaukee, Wisconsin 53202

Variety of filmstrip sets on biblical subjects. Free catalogue.

THESIS TAPES

    P.O. Box 11724
    Pittsburgh, Pennsylvania 15228

"Faith Alive" series of cassettes. Free catalogue.

UNITED CHURCH OF CHRIST

    Audio-Visual Office
    1505 Race Street
    Philadelphia, Pennsylvania 19102

Variety of filmstrips, many on New Testament subjects. Free catalogue.